EYEWITNESS
OCEAN

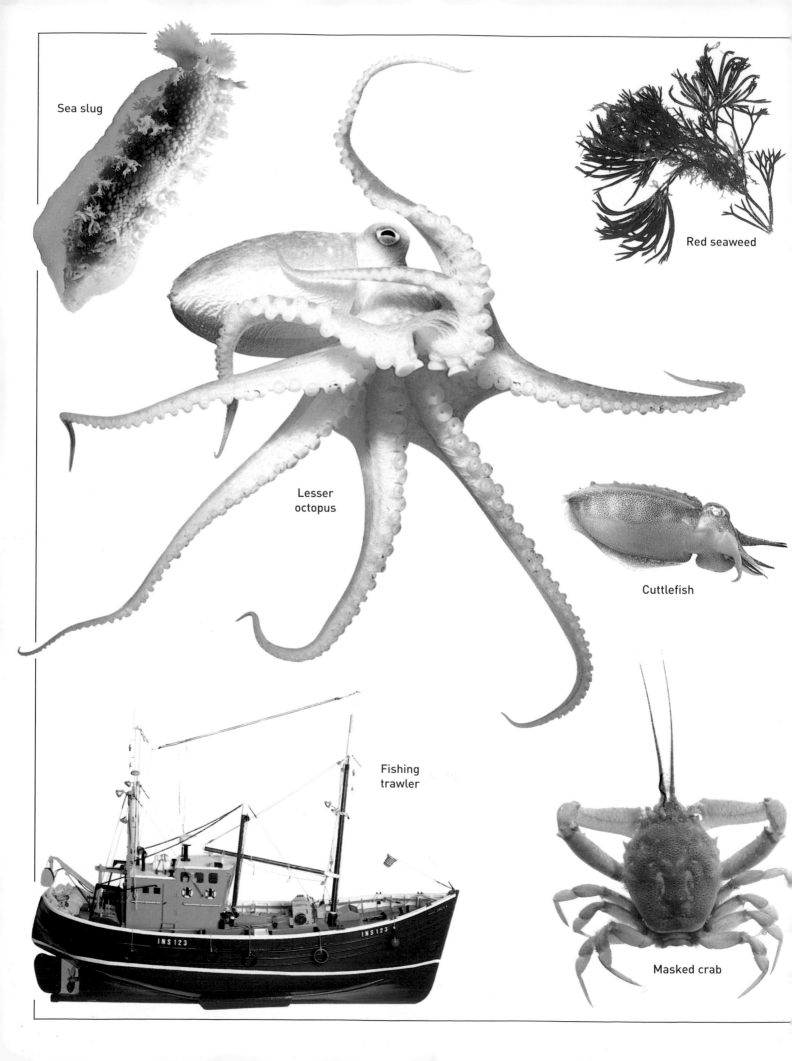

Sea slug

Red seaweed

Lesser octopus

Cuttlefish

Fishing trawler

Masked crab

Boar fish

EYEWITNESS
OCEAN

Written by
DR. MIRANDA MACQUITTY

Photographed by
FRANK GREENAWAY

European
spiny lobster

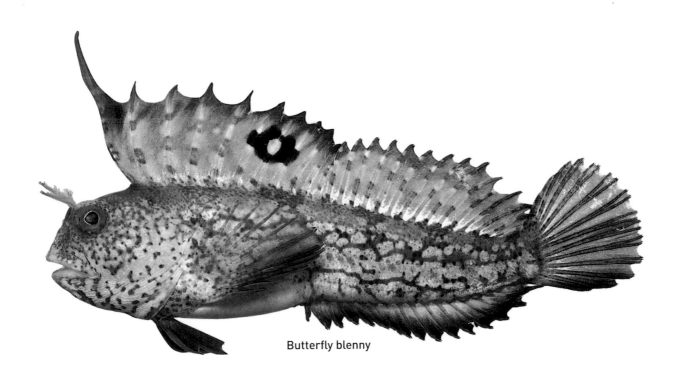
Butterfly blenny

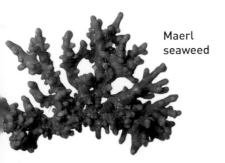
Maerl
seaweed

Common
sea urchin

Common starfish

Microscope used in the late 1800s

Prepared slides

Common sunstar

Dead man's fingers

Parchment worm inside its tube

Red cushion star

Mussel shells

Red cushion star

Victorian collection of shells

Preserving jar containing a Norwegian lobster

DK

LONDON, NEW YORK,
MELBOURNE, MUNICH, AND DELHI

Project editor Marion Dent
Art editor Jane Tetzlaff
Managing editor Gillian Denton
Managing art editor Julia Harris
Research Céline Carez
Picture research Kathy Lockley
Production Catherine Semark

RELAUNCH EDITION (DK UK)
Editor Ashwin Khurana
US editor Margaret Parrish
Senior designers Rachael Grady, Spencer Holbrook
Managing editor Gareth Jones
Managing art editor Philip Letsu
Publisher Andrew Macintyre
Producer, preproduction Adam Stoneham
Senior producer Charlotte Cade
Jacket editor Maud Whatley
Jacket designer Laura Brim
Jacket design development manager Sophia MTT
Publishing director Jonathan Metcalf
Associate publishing director Liz Wheeler
Art director Phil Ormerod

RELAUNCH EDITION (DK INDIA)
Editor Surbhi Nayyar Kapoor
Art editors Deep Shikha Walia, Vikas Chauhan
Senior DTP designer Harish Aggarwal
DTP designers Anita Yadav, Pawan Kumar
Managing editor Alka Thakur Hazarika
Managing art editor Romi Chakraborty
CTS manager Balwant Singh
Jacket editorial manager Saloni Talwar
Jacket designers Govind Mittal, Suhita Dharamjit, Vidit Vashisht

First American Edition, 1995
This American Edition, 2014
Published in the United States by DK Publishing
4th floor, 345 Hudson Street
New York, New York 10014

14 15 16 17 18   10 9 8 7 6 5 4 3 2 1
196429—07/14

A catalog record for this book is available from
the Library of Congress.

ISBN 978-1-4654-2054-1 (Paperback)
ISBN 978-1-4654-2096-1 (ALB)

DK books are available at special discounts when purchased
in bulk for sales promotions, premiums, fund-raising, or
educational use. For details, contact:
DK Publishing Special Markets, 345 Hudson Street,
New York, New York 10014 or SpecialSale@dk.com.

Color reproduction by Alta Image Ltd., London, UK
Printed and bound by South China Printing Co. Ltd., China

Discover more at
www.dk.com

Contents

Squat lobster

Oceans of the past

Today's oceans started to take shape in the last 200 million years of Earth's 4.6-billion-year existence. But long before, as the early planet cooled, water vapor in the atmosphere condensed, clouds formed, and rain filled the oceans. Water also came from space, in icy comets. As the land masses drifted, new oceans opened up, old oceans disappeared, and ocean life changed, too. Simple organisms first appeared in the oceans 3.5 billion years ago, followed by ever more complex life-forms.

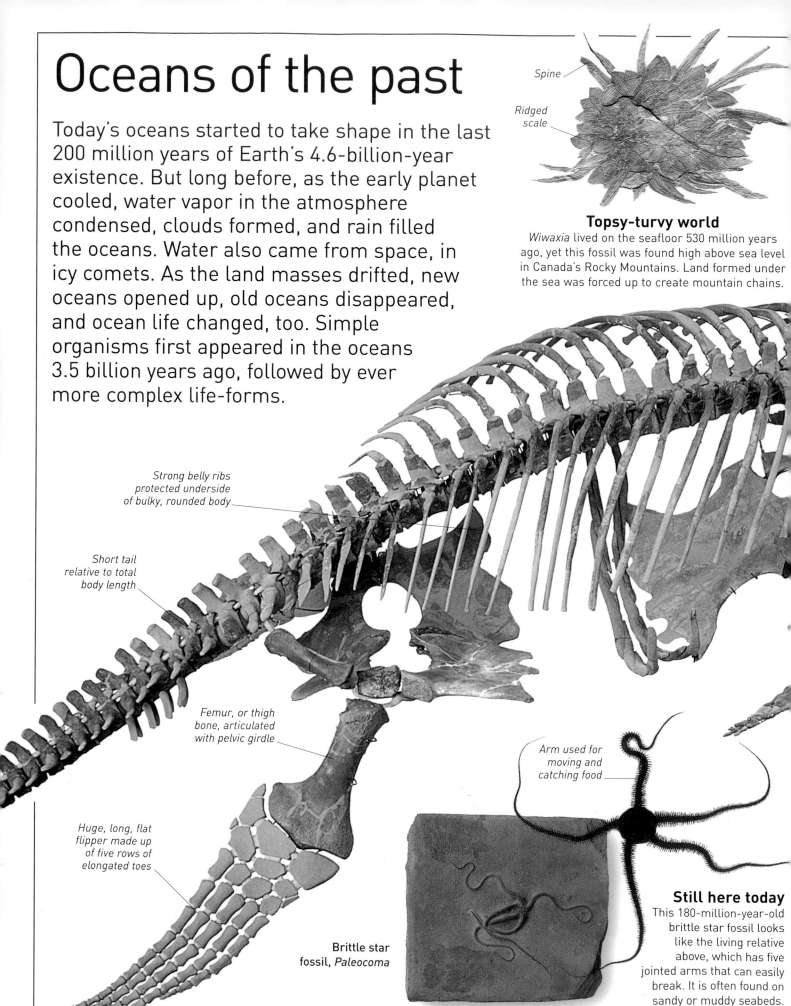

Spine

Ridged scale

Topsy-turvy world
Wiwaxia lived on the seafloor 530 million years ago, yet this fossil was found high above sea level in Canada's Rocky Mountains. Land formed under the sea was forced up to create mountain chains.

Strong belly ribs protected underside of bulky, rounded body

Short tail relative to total body length

Femur, or thigh bone, articulated with pelvic girdle

Huge, long, flat flipper made up of five rows of elongated toes

Brittle star fossil, *Paleocoma*

Arm used for moving and catching food

Still here today
This 180-million-year-old brittle star fossil looks like the living relative above, which has five jointed arms that can easily break. It is often found on sandy or muddy seabeds.

Ancient coral

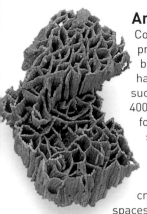

Corals were well preserved in rocks because of their hard skeletons, such as this 400-million-year-old fossil coral. The skeleton of each tiny coral animal joined that of its neighbor to create chains with spaces between them.

Changing oceans

A giant ocean, Panthalassa, surrounded the supercontinent Pangaea (1), 290–240 mya (million years ago). At the end of this period, many kinds of marine life became extinct. Pangaea split apart, around the Tethys Sea.

Continental drift

The North Atlantic formed 208–146 mya (2). The South Atlantic and Indian oceans began to form 146–65 mya (3). The continents continued to drift 1.64 mya (4), and the oceans are still changing shape today.

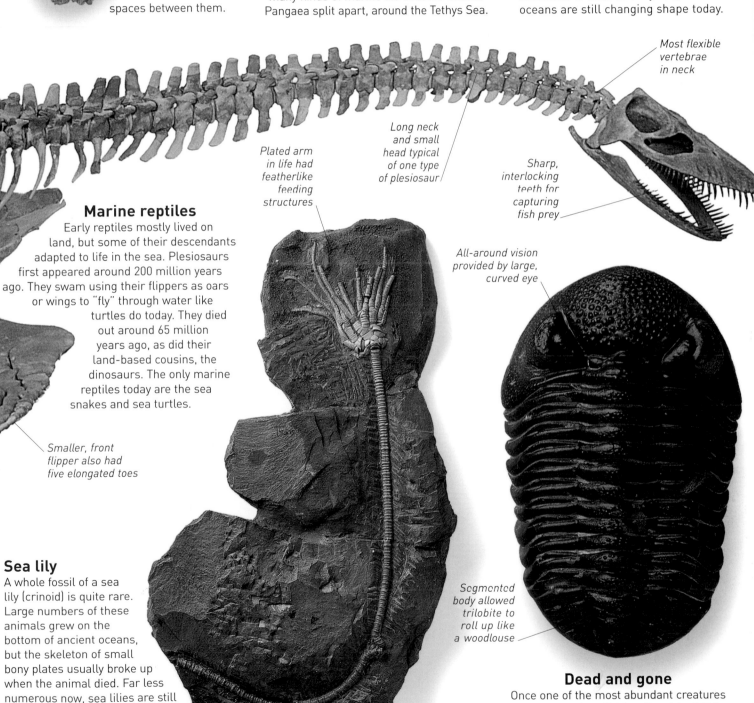

Most flexible vertebrae in neck

Long neck and small head typical of one type of plesiosaur

Plated arm in life had featherlike feeding structures

Sharp, interlocking teeth for capturing fish prey

Marine reptiles

Early reptiles mostly lived on land, but some of their descendants adapted to life in the sea. Plesiosaurs first appeared around 200 million years ago. They swam using their flippers as oars or wings to "fly" through water like turtles do today. They died out around 65 million years ago, as did their land-based cousins, the dinosaurs. The only marine reptiles today are the sea snakes and sea turtles.

Smaller, front flipper also had five elongated toes

All-around vision provided by large, curved eye

Sea lily

A whole fossil of a sea lily (crinoid) is quite rare. Large numbers of these animals grew on the bottom of ancient oceans, but the skeleton of small bony plates usually broke up when the animal died. Far less numerous now, sea lilies are still found living below 330 ft (100 m), usually anchored to the seabed. Arms around their mouths trap small particles of food drifting by.

Segmented body allowed trilobite to roll up like a woodlouse

Long, flexible stem anchored crinoid in sea-bed gardens

Dead and gone

Once one of the most abundant creatures in ancient seas, trilobites flourished 510–250 million years ago. They had jointed limbs and an external skeleton like insects and crustaceans (such as crabs and lobsters).

Oceans today

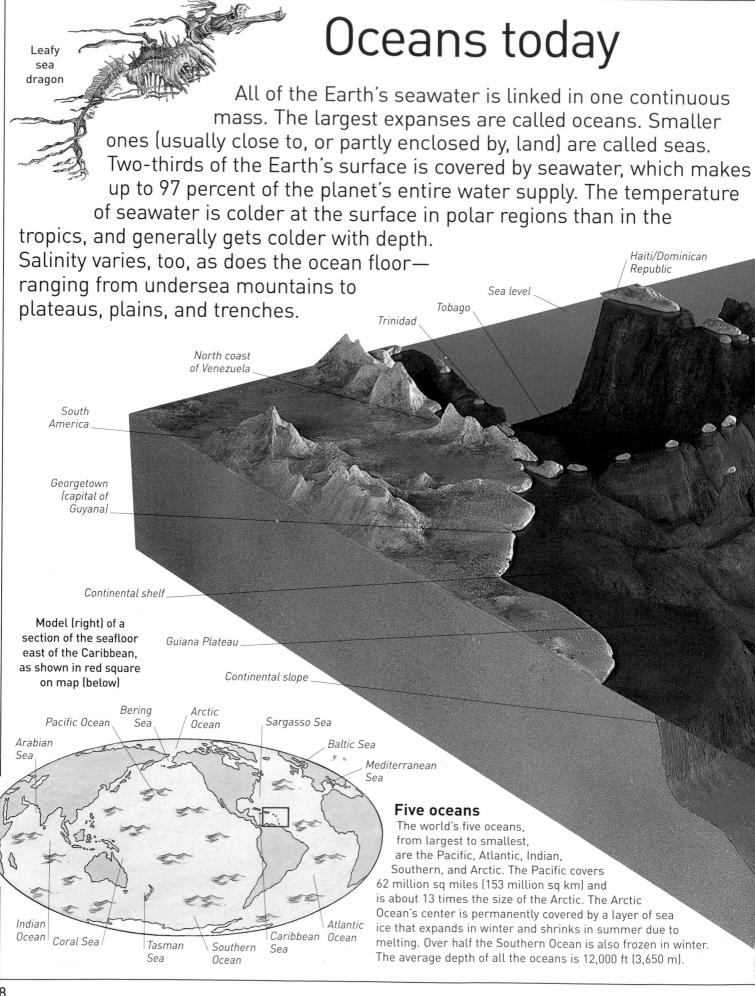

Leafy sea dragon

All of the Earth's seawater is linked in one continuous mass. The largest expanses are called oceans. Smaller ones (usually close to, or partly enclosed by, land) are called seas. Two-thirds of the Earth's surface is covered by seawater, which makes up to 97 percent of the planet's entire water supply. The temperature of seawater is colder at the surface in polar regions than in the tropics, and generally gets colder with depth. Salinity varies, too, as does the ocean floor— ranging from undersea mountains to plateaus, plains, and trenches.

Haiti/Dominican Republic

Sea level

Tobago

Trinidad

North coast of Venezuela

South America

Georgetown (capital of Guyana)

Continental shelf

Model (right) of a section of the seafloor east of the Caribbean, as shown in red square on map (below)

Guiana Plateau

Continental slope

Pacific Ocean

Bering Sea

Arctic Ocean

Sargasso Sea

Arabian Sea

Baltic Sea

Mediterranean Sea

Indian Ocean

Coral Sea

Tasman Sea

Southern Ocean

Caribbean Sea

Atlantic Ocean

Five oceans

The world's five oceans, from largest to smallest, are the Pacific, Atlantic, Indian, Southern, and Arctic. The Pacific covers 62 million sq miles (153 million sq km) and is about 13 times the size of the Arctic. The Arctic Ocean's center is permanently covered by a layer of sea ice that expands in winter and shrinks in summer due to melting. Over half the Southern Ocean is also frozen in winter. The average depth of all the oceans is 12,000 ft (3,650 m).

Sea or lake?

Surrounded by desert, the Dead Sea is saltier than any ocean because the water that drains into it evaporates in the hot sun; the body can float on the salts left behind. The Dead Sea is a lake, not a true sea, as it has no channel linking it to the ocean.

Floating on the Dead Sea

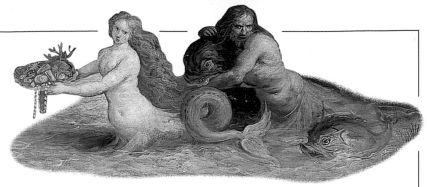

God of the waters

Neptune, the Roman god of the sea, is often shown riding a dolphin and carrying a three-pronged spear (trident). He was also thought to control freshwater supplies.

Disappearing act

The gigantic tectonic plates on Earth's crust move like a conveyor belt. New areas of ocean floor form at spreading centers, and old areas sink below trenches where one oceanic plate is forced under another (subduction).

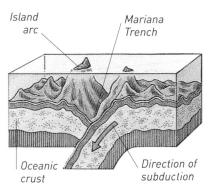

Formation of Mariana Trench

Island arc *Mariana Trench* *Oceanic crust* *Direction of subduction*

Hatteras Abyssal Plain

Puerto Rico Trench

Nares Abyssal Plain

Mid-Atlantic Ridge

Kane Fracture Zone

Vema Fracture Zone

Demerara Abyssal Plain

The ocean floor

This model shows the Atlantic Ocean off northeast South America. Off this coast is the continental shelf, under relatively shallow water about 650 ft (200 m) deep. The shelf is about 125 miles (200 km) wide here, but it is up to 1,000 miles (1,600 km) wide off northern Asia. From there, the ocean floor drops steeply, to form the continental slope. Sediments eroded from the land and carried by rivers accumulate at the bottom of this slope. The ocean floor then opens out in virtually flat abyssal plains. Deep trenches, such as the Puerto Rican Trench, can form where one of Earth's tectonic plates slides past another. An arc of volcanic islands has also been created where the North American Plate is forced under the Caribbean Plate.

Ocean life

Oceans are home to some of the most diverse life on Earth. Animals live either on the seabed or in mid-water, where they swim or float. Plants are only found in the sunlit zone where there is enough light for them to grow, and they are anchored to the seafloor or drifting in the water. Animals are found at all depths, but are most abundant in the sunlit zone where food is plentiful. Some animals move from one zone to another, to surface for air or to find more food. Over 90 percent of all species dwell on the seafloor. One rock can house 10 major groups, such as corals and sponges.

Bloody Henry starfish

Common sunstar

Shore life

Often found on the shore at low tide, starfish also live in deeper water. Sea life on the shore must either be tough enough to withstand drying out, or shelter in rock pools.

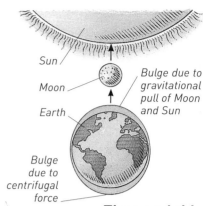

Sun

Moon

Earth

Bulge due to gravitational pull of Moon and Sun

Bulge due to centrifugal force

Time and tide

Tides are caused by the gravitational pull of the Moon on the Earth's seawater on one side of the planet and by centrifugal force on the opposite side. As the Earth spins around over 24 hours, the bulges (high tides) usually occur twice a day in any one place. The highest and lowest tides (spring tides) occur when the Moon and Sun are in line, causing the greatest gravitational pull.

Speedy squid

One of the most common animals in the sea, squid often swim in schools for protection. Built like streamlined torpedoes, they can swim quickly.

Inside squid's soft body is a horny, penlike shell

Funnel expels jet of water for moving in water

Tentacles reach out to grasp food

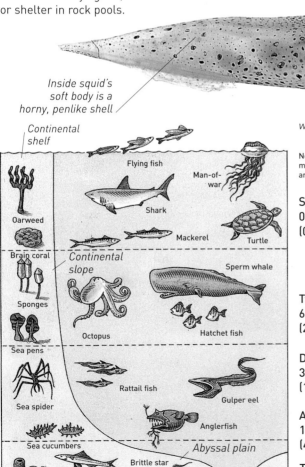

Continental shelf

Flying fish

Man-of-war

Shark

Mackerel

Turtle

Oarweed

Brain coral

Continental slope

Sperm whale

Sponges

Octopus

Hatchet fish

Sea pens

Rattail fish

Gulper eel

Sea spider

Anglerfish

Sea cucumbers

Abyssal plain

Flower-basket sponge

Brittle star

Tripod fish

Deep-sea anemone

Note: Neither the marine life nor zones are drawn to scale

Sunlit zone
0–650 ft
(0–200 m)

Twilight zone
650–3,300 ft
(200–1,000 m)

Dark zone
3,300–13,000 ft
(1,000–4,000 m)

Abyss
13,000–20,000 ft
(4,000–6,000 m)

Trench
Over 20,000 ft
(6,000 m)

Deep-sea cat shark grows to only 20 in (50 cm) long

The ocean's zones

The ocean is divided into zones. In the sunlit zone, there is plenty of light, considerable water movement, and seasonal changes in temperature. Beneath this is the twilight zone, where there is little light and temperatures drop rapidly with depth to about 41°F (5°C). Deeper yet is the dark zone, where there is no light and temperatures drop to about 34–36°F (1–2°C). Even deeper is the abyss and then the trenches. There are also zones on the seabed, from the continental shelf to continental slope, abyssal plains, and trenches.

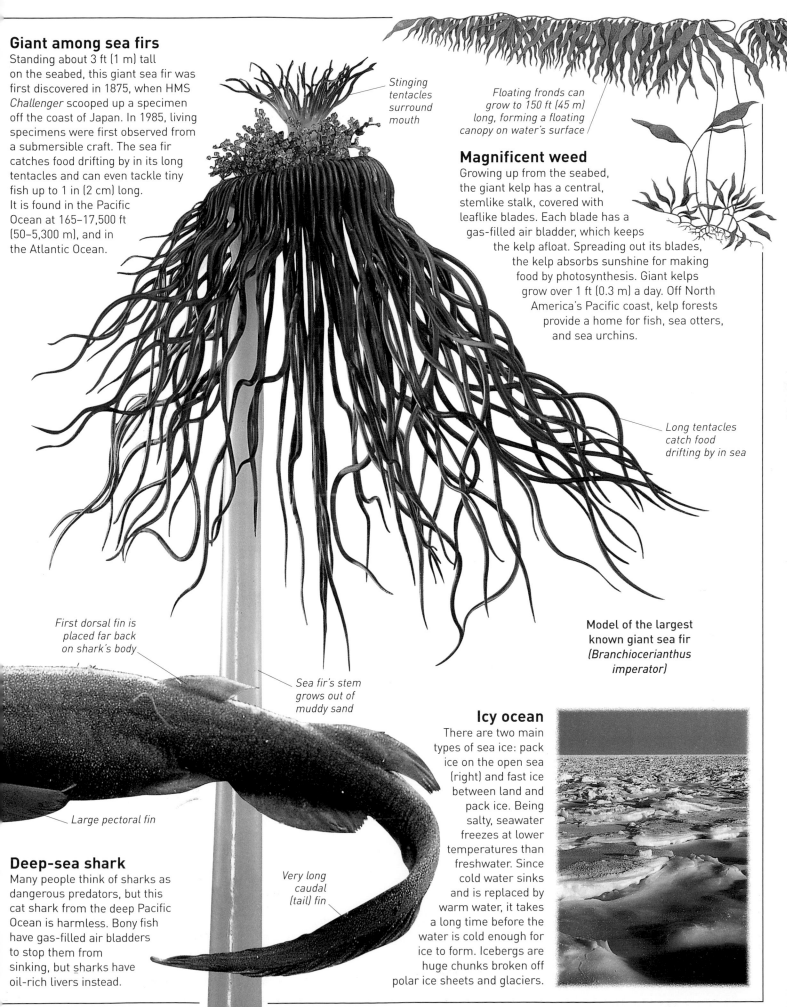

Giant among sea firs
Standing about 3 ft (1 m) tall on the seabed, this giant sea fir was first discovered in 1875, when HMS *Challenger* scooped up a specimen off the coast of Japan. In 1985, living specimens were first observed from a submersible craft. The sea fir catches food drifting by in its long tentacles and can even tackle tiny fish up to 1 in (2 cm) long. It is found in the Pacific Ocean at 165–17,500 ft (50–5,300 m), and in the Atlantic Ocean.

Stinging tentacles surround mouth

Floating fronds can grow to 150 ft (45 m) long, forming a floating canopy on water's surface

Magnificent weed
Growing up from the seabed, the giant kelp has a central, stemlike stalk, covered with leaflike blades. Each blade has a gas-filled air bladder, which keeps the kelp afloat. Spreading out its blades, the kelp absorbs sunshine for making food by photosynthesis. Giant kelps grow over 1 ft (0.3 m) a day. Off North America's Pacific coast, kelp forests provide a home for fish, sea otters, and sea urchins.

Long tentacles catch food drifting by in sea

First dorsal fin is placed far back on shark's body

Sea fir's stem grows out of muddy sand

Model of the largest known giant sea fir (*Branchiocerianthus imperator*)

Large pectoral fin

Deep-sea shark
Many people think of sharks as dangerous predators, but this cat shark from the deep Pacific Ocean is harmless. Bony fish have gas-filled air bladders to stop them from sinking, but sharks have oil-rich livers instead.

Very long caudal (tail) fin

Icy ocean
There are two main types of sea ice: pack ice on the open sea (right) and fast ice between land and pack ice. Being salty, seawater freezes at lower temperatures than freshwater. Since cold water sinks and is replaced by warm water, it takes a long time before the water is cold enough for ice to form. Icebergs are huge chunks broken off polar ice sheets and glaciers.

Waves and weather

Seawater is always moving. Winds drive the waves and major surface currents are driven by the prevailing winds. Surface and deep-water currents help to modify the world's climate by moving cold water from polar regions toward the tropics, and vice versa. Heat from the oceans creates air movement. The ocean heats up more slowly than the land by day. Cool air above the water blows in, replacing warm air above the land. The reverse happens at night.

Down the spout
Water spouts suck up water when whirling air drops down from a storm cloud to the sea.

Rivers of the sea
Currents are huge masses of water moving through the oceans. The course that currents follow is not precisely the same as the trade winds and westerlies, because currents are deflected by land and the Coriolis Force produced by Earth's rotation. The latter causes currents to shift to the right in the northern hemisphere and to the left in the southern.

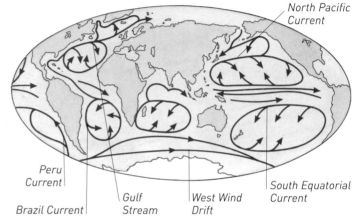

North Pacific Current

Peru Current

Brazil Current

Gulf Stream

West Wind Drift

South Equatorial Current

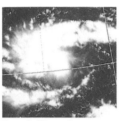

Day 2: Thunderstorms as swirling cloud mass

Day 4: Winds have increased in intensity

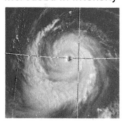

Day 7: Strong winds

A hurricane is born
These satellite images show a hurricane forming, from a swirling cloud mass to ferocious winds over seven days.

Strongest winds of up to 220 mph (360 kph) occur just outside the eye

Ice forms at the very tops of clouds

Hurricanes are enormous— some can be 500 miles (800 km) across

Warm, moist air spirals up around eye inside hurricane

Torrential rains fall from clouds

Energy to drive storm comes from a warm ocean at 80°F (27°C) or more

Hurricane!
Also known as typhoons, hurricanes form in the tropics where warm, moist air rises up from the ocean's surface, creating storm clouds. As more air spirals upward, the energy released fuels stronger winds that whirl around the eye (a calm area of extreme low pressure). Hurricanes cause devastation over land. Away from the ocean, they die out.

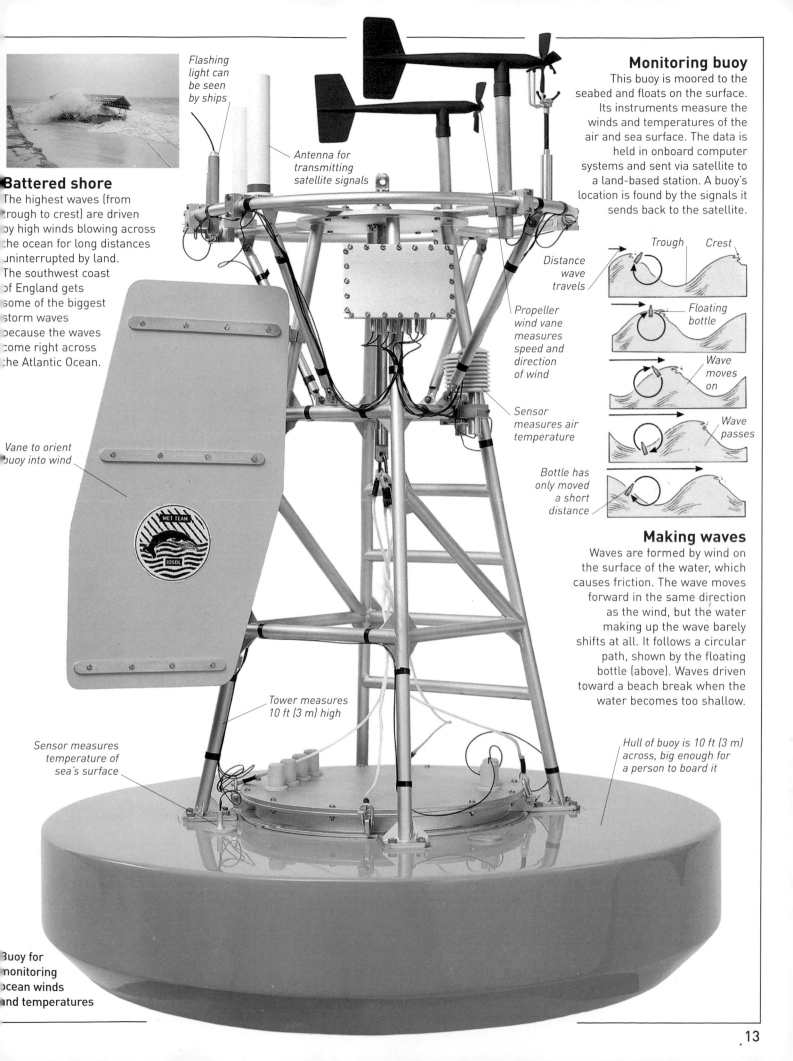

Battered shore

The highest waves (from trough to crest) are driven by high winds blowing across the ocean for long distances uninterrupted by land. The southwest coast of England gets some of the biggest storm waves because the waves come right across the Atlantic Ocean.

Flashing light can be seen by ships

Antenna for transmitting satellite signals

Vane to orient buoy into wind

MET TEAM
IOSDL

Monitoring buoy

This buoy is moored to the seabed and floats on the surface. Its instruments measure the winds and temperatures of the air and sea surface. The data is held in onboard computer systems and sent via satellite to a land-based station. A buoy's location is found by the signals it sends back to the satellite.

Distance wave travels

Trough   Crest

Floating bottle

Wave moves on

Wave passes

Bottle has only moved a short distance

Propeller wind vane measures speed and direction of wind

Sensor measures air temperature

Making waves

Waves are formed by wind on the surface of the water, which causes friction. The wave moves forward in the same direction as the wind, but the water making up the wave barely shifts at all. It follows a circular path, shown by the floating bottle (above). Waves driven toward a beach break when the water becomes too shallow.

Tower measures 10 ft (3 m) high

Hull of buoy is 10 ft (3 m) across, big enough for a person to board it

Sensor measures temperature of sea's surface

Buoy for monitoring ocean winds and temperatures

Sandy and muddy

In shallow coastal waters, sand and mud are washed from the land to the edge of the continental shelf. Vast stretches of the seafloor look like underwater deserts. Finer-grained mud settles in places where the water is calmer. Without rocks, there are fewer seaweeds to provide shelter, so animals that venture onto the surface are exposed to predators. Many of these creatures avoid them by hiding in the soft seabed. All the animals shown here live in the coastal waters of the Atlantic Ocean.

Tough papery tube protects soft worm inside

Worm can grow up to 16 in (40 cm) long

Bulky body 4 in (10 cm) long is covered by dense mat of fine hairs

Coarse, shiny bristles help it to move along seabed

Bristling beauty

The sea mouse plows through muddy sand on the seabed, eating any dead animals it finds. The rainbow-colored spines help propel this chunky worm and may deter hungry fish. Keeping its rear end out of the sand brings in fresh seawater to help it breathe.

Light color helps it merge into sand

Thick trunk looks like a peanut when whole body retracts

Surface of plump, unsegmented body feels rough

Poisonous spines on first dorsal fin

Peanut worm

Many groups of worms live in the sea. This is one of 320 types of sipunculid—or peanut worm—that hide in the sand or in empty sea shells. A stretchy front part can retract into the thicker trunk.

Front part can also retract

Poisonous spine on front of gill cover

High-set eye allows all-around vision

Mouth surrounded by tentacles

Wary weever

When a weever fish is buried in sand, the eyes on top of its head help it see what is going on. Poisonous spines provide extra defense and can inflict nasty wounds if a weever is stepped on or caught in a fishing net.

Flat fish

Flounders cruise along the sea looking for food. They nibble the tops off peacock worms.

Fan-shaped flaps beat to let food pass along worm's body

Parapodia, or feetlike flaps

Feelerlike palps (sense organs)

Red seaweed grows on whitish ends of tube

Tentacles fringed with fine hairs

Parapodia

Mouth

Parchment worm outside its tube

Fan-shaped flap

When buried, the tube is often U-shaped

Parapodia

A look inside

The parchment worm lives in a U-shaped tube with ends that stick out above the mud's surface. It draws water containing food into its tube. Fan-shaped flaps waft the water along. Food is trapped in a slimy net that is rolled up and passed toward the mouth. A new net is then made and the process repeated.

Tentacles disappear quickly into tube if danger is present

Like a peacock's fan

A crown of tentacles helps peacock worms feed and breathe. As water passes through the tentacles, particles in the water are passed down rows of tiny beating hairs into the mouth in the crown's center. Larger particles help make the tube.

Peacock worm can be 10 in (25 cm) long

Tube made of mud and sand particles bound together with worm's hardened slime

Soft seabed

On a soft seabed, few animals are visible because most of them live buried in the sand. You may spot a crab's feathery antennae or a clam's siphon, which help these animals get a clean supply of oxygenated water to breathe. Some fish visit the soft seabed to feed on burrowing clams. Other animals are found among sea grasses. These flowering plants are food for many animals.

Tough skin protects dugong

Docile dugong
Found in shallow tropical waters, this shy, gentle mammal feeds on sea grasses growing in the soft seabed and digs out their roots.

Anemone-like polyp unfurls when feeding

Elegant pen
Shaped like a writing quill, this sea pen lives in the soft seabed. Rows of tiny polyps unfurl on each side of its body to capture small animals drifting by. Sea pens glow in the dark if they are disturbed.

This sea pen can grow to 8 in (20 cm) in height

Long dorsal fin runs along almost whole length of body

Shell boat
In Botticelli's *The Birth of Venus*, the Roman goddess rises from the sea in a huge scallop shell. The real shell would fit in your hand.

Red band fish
This fish usually lives in burrows in the soft seabed, as far down as 660 ft (200 m). It is also found swimming among sea grasses. When out of its burrow, the fish swims by passing waves down its body. It feeds on small animals.

Long anal fin

Red band fish may grow to 28 in (70 cm) in length

Stem of sea pen anchors in sandy seabed

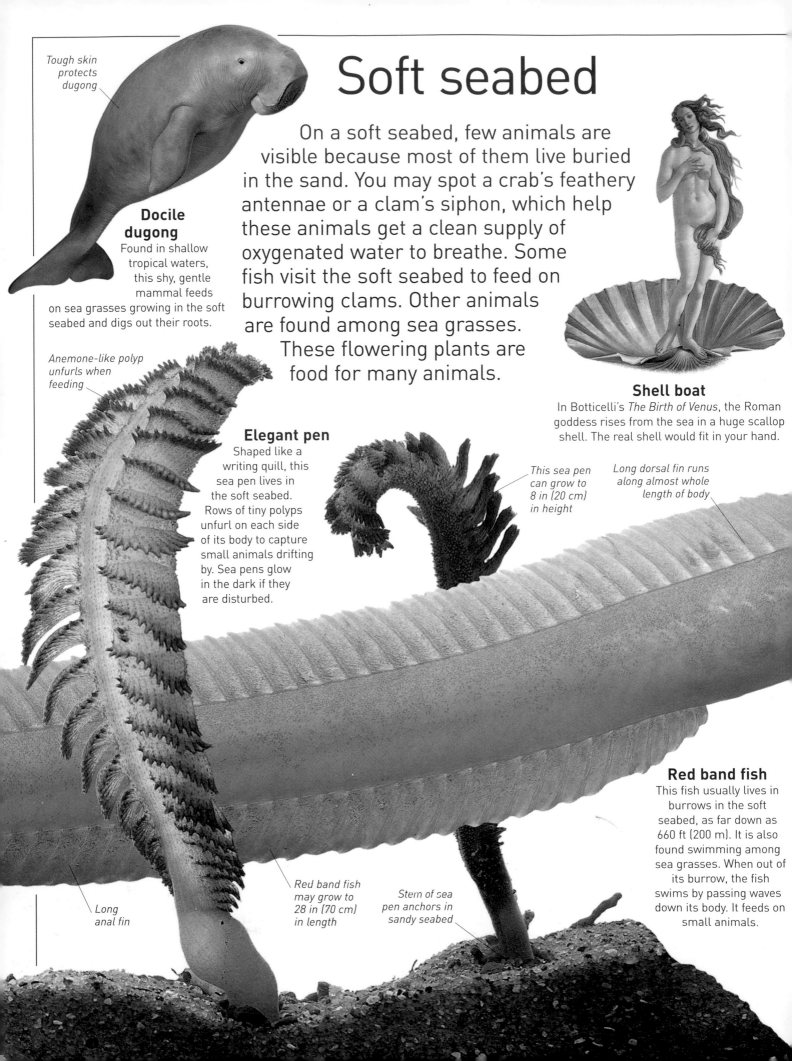

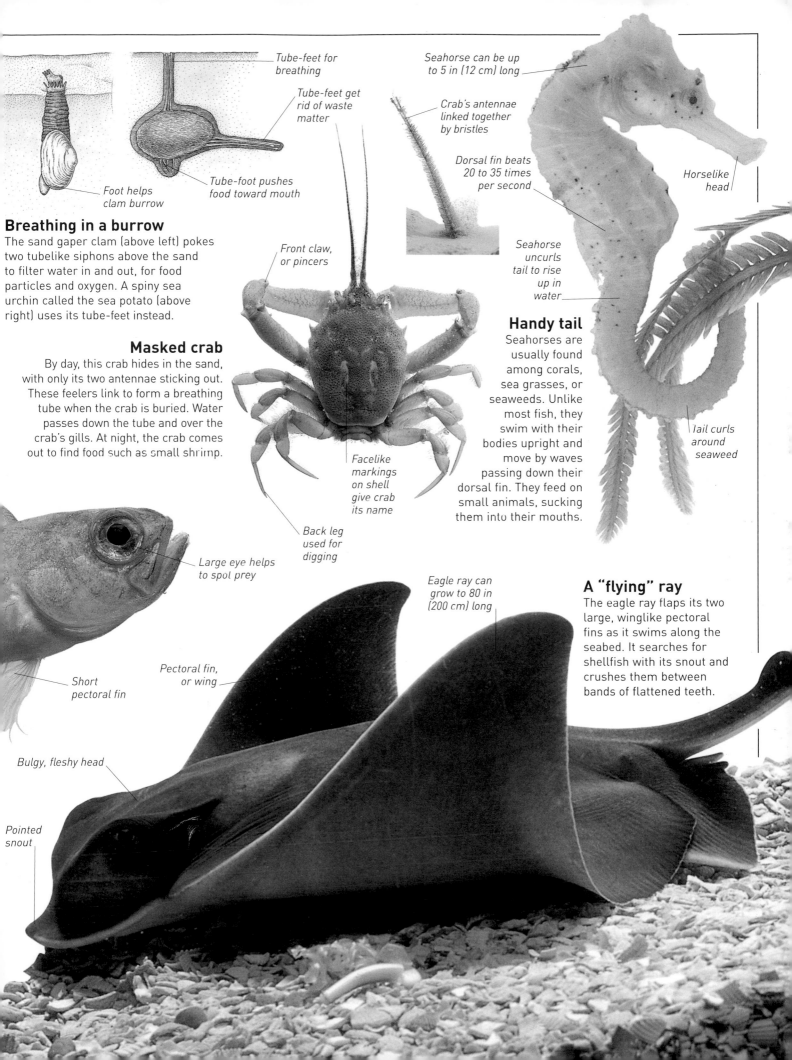

Tube-feet for breathing

Tube-feet get rid of waste matter

Foot helps clam burrow

Tube-foot pushes food toward mouth

Breathing in a burrow

The sand gaper clam (above left) pokes two tubelike siphons above the sand to filter water in and out, for food particles and oxygen. A spiny sea urchin called the sea potato (above right) uses its tube-feet instead.

Masked crab

By day, this crab hides in the sand, with only its two antennae sticking out. These feelers link to form a breathing tube when the crab is buried. Water passes down the tube and over the crab's gills. At night, the crab comes out to find food such as small shrimp.

Front claw, or pincers

Facelike markings on shell give crab its name

Back leg used for digging

Crab's antennae linked together by bristles

Dorsal fin beats 20 to 35 times per second

Seahorse can be up to 5 in (12 cm) long

Horselike head

Seahorse uncurls tail to rise up in water

Tail curls around seaweed

Handy tail

Seahorses are usually found among corals, sea grasses, or seaweeds. Unlike most fish, they swim with their bodies upright and move by waves passing down their dorsal fin. They feed on small animals, sucking them into their mouths.

Large eye helps to spot prey

Short pectoral fin

Bulgy, fleshy head

Pointed snout

Pectoral fin, or wing

Eagle ray can grow to 80 in (200 cm) long

A "flying" ray

The eagle ray flaps its two large, winglike pectoral fins as it swims along the seabed. It searches for shellfish with its snout and crushes them between bands of flattened teeth.

Rocks underwater

Rocks make up the seabed in coastal waters, where currents sweep away any sand and mud. Animals must cling to rocks, find crevices to hide in, or shelter in seaweeds. Piddocks (clams) and some sea urchins can bore into solid rock to make their homes. Some other animals hide under small stones lodged in the soft seabed, but where masses of loose pebbles roll around, animals and seaweeds can be crushed. Some animals can survive at the water's edge, especially in rock pools, but many need to stay submerged.

Sea urchin boring into rocks

Piddock

Rock borers

Some sea urchins use their spines and teeth to bore holes in rock. Using its muscular foot, the piddock twists and turns to drill with the tip of its shell and hold onto its burrow.

Spiny lobster

European spiny lobsters have small pincers and are restricted to eating soft prey such as worms, or devouring dead animals. They live among rocks, hiding in crevices by day, but venture out over the seabed to find food al night.

Dorsal fin has eyespot to frighten predators

Beautiful butterfly

Blennies, small fish living in shallow water, often rest on the seafloor and hide in small spaces. They lay their eggs in sheltered places, such as old bottles, and guard them from predators.

Spiny shell helps deter predators

Delicate claw on tip of walking leg

European spiny lobster, also known as a crayfish or crawfish

Leg used for walking

Tail can be flapped so lobster can swim backward

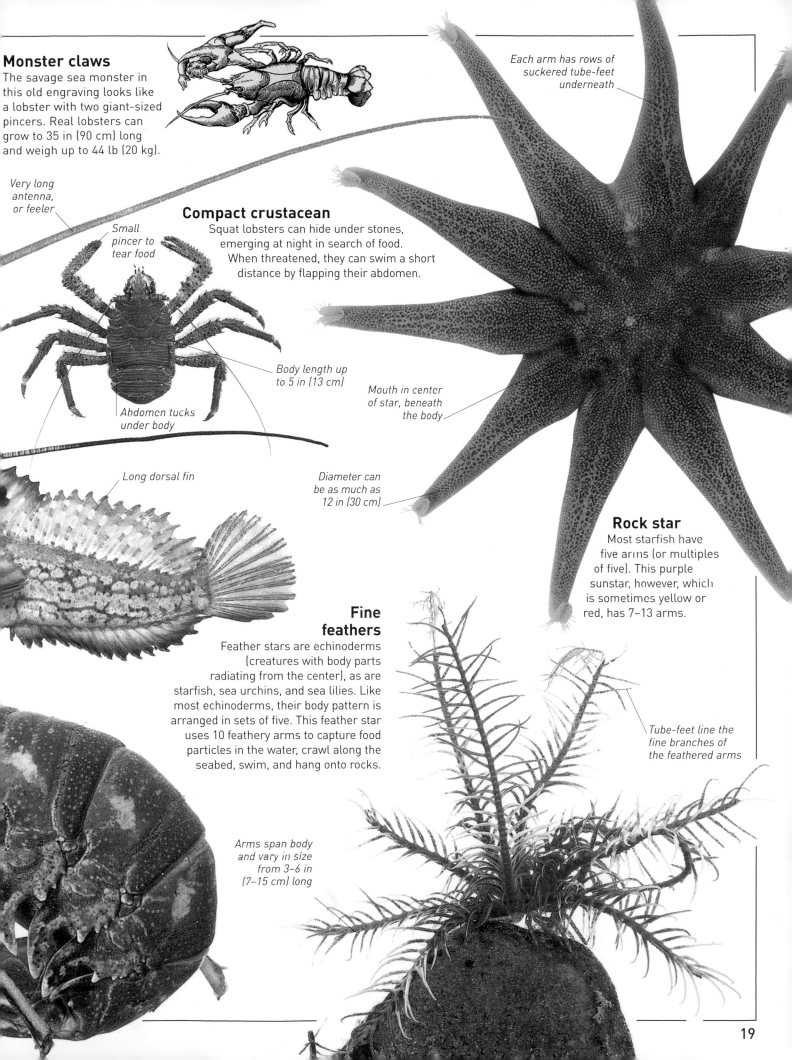

Monster claws

The savage sea monster in this old engraving looks like a lobster with two giant-sized pincers. Real lobsters can grow to 35 in (90 cm) long and weigh up to 44 lb (20 kg).

Very long antenna, or feeler

Small pincer to tear food

Compact crustacean

Squat lobsters can hide under stones, emerging at night in search of food. When threatened, they can swim a short distance by flapping their abdomen.

Body length up to 5 in (13 cm)

Abdomen tucks under body

Each arm has rows of suckered tube-feet underneath

Mouth in center of star, beneath the body

Long dorsal fin

Diameter can be as much as 12 in (30 cm)

Rock star

Most starfish have five arms (or multiples of five). This purple sunstar, however, which is sometimes yellow or red, has 7–13 arms.

Fine feathers

Feather stars are echinoderms (creatures with body parts radiating from the center), as are starfish, sea urchins, and sea lilies. Like most echinoderms, their body pattern is arranged in sets of five. This feather star uses 10 feathery arms to capture food particles in the water, crawl along the seabed, swim, and hang onto rocks.

Tube-feet line the fine branches of the feathered arms

Arms span body and vary in size from 3–6 in (7–15 cm) long

A type of brown seaweed (kelp) from the Pacific Ocean

On the rocks

In shallow, cool waters above rocky seabeds, forests of kelp (large brown seaweeds) are home to many sea creatures. Fish swim among the giant fronds. Sea otters wrap themselves in kelp while sleeping on the surface. Tightly gripping the rocks, the kelp's rootlike anchor (holdfast) houses hordes of tiny creatures, such as worms and mites. Anchored to rocks, mussels provide homes for some animals between or within their shells.

Marine mammal

Sea otters swim and rest among giant kelp fronds along North America's Pacific coast. They smash shellfish open on a rock balanced on their chest.

Anchored algae

Holdfasts of the large, tough, brown algae called kelp keep it firmly anchored to the rocks.

Holdfast of oarweed kelp

Holdfast must be strong, since some kelp can grow to hundreds of feet long

Scaleless body is covered with small, warty bumps

Hold on tight

Lumpsuckers cling to rocks with suckerlike fins on their bellies. They come into shallow water to breed and the father guards the eggs.

Juvenile lumpsucker

Each sturdy, blunt finger measures at least 1 in (3 cm) across

Fleshy fingers supported by many, tiny, hard splinters

White, anemone-like polyp captures food from fast currents

Gills

Dead man's fingers

Growing on rocks, the colonies of this soft coral consist of many polyps (feeding bodies) within a fleshy, orange or white base.

Microscopic sea mat

The lacy-looking growth on the kelp's surface (left) is a colony of bryozoans, or moss animals. Each little compartment houses one of these animals, which come out to capture food in their tiny tentacles. Other kinds of moss animal grow upward, looking like seaweeds or corals. Between the sea mats, a blue-rayed limpet grazes on the kelp's surface.

Sea slug

Many sea slugs are meat-eaters. This slug lives on the soft coral known as dead man's fingers. Sea slug eggs hatch into swimming young, which then settle and turn into adults.

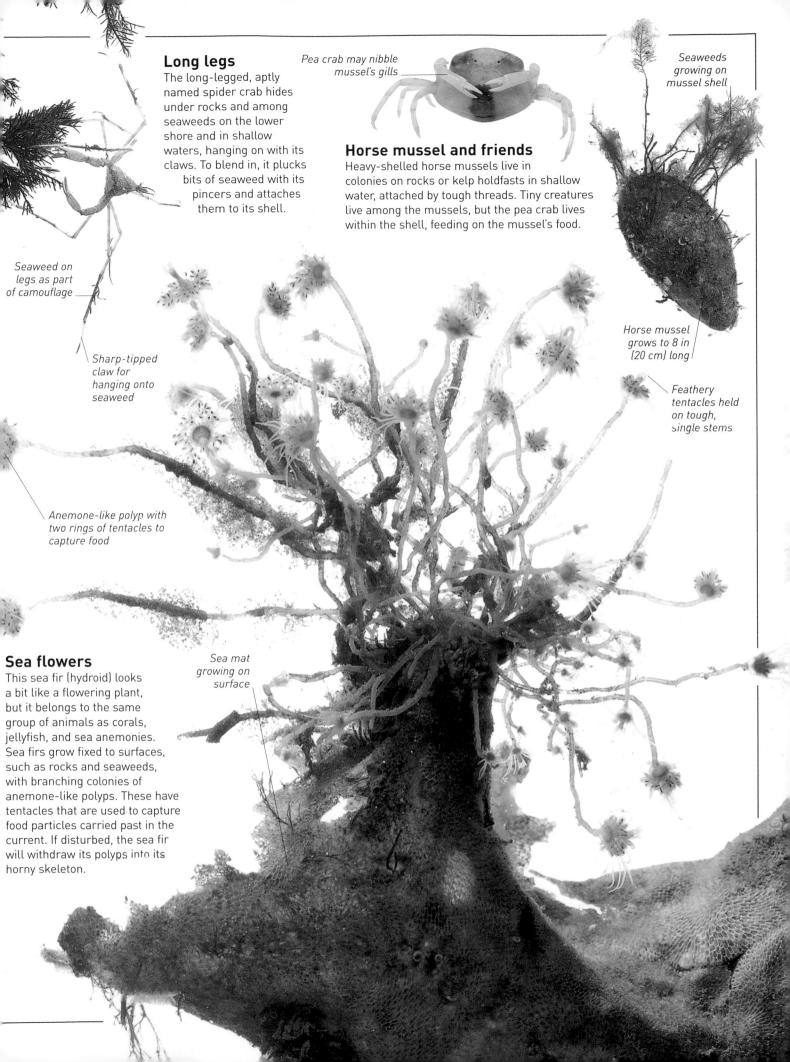

Long legs

The long-legged, aptly named spider crab hides under rocks and among seaweeds on the lower shore and in shallow waters, hanging on with its claws. To blend in, it plucks bits of seaweed with its pincers and attaches them to its shell.

Pea crab may nibble mussel's gills

Seaweeds growing on mussel shell

Horse mussel and friends

Heavy-shelled horse mussels live in colonies on rocks or kelp holdfasts in shallow water, attached by tough threads. Tiny creatures live among the mussels, but the pea crab lives within the shell, feeding on the mussel's food.

Seaweed on legs as part of camouflage

Sharp-tipped claw for hanging onto seaweed

Horse mussel grows to 8 in (20 cm) long

Feathery tentacles held on tough, single stems

Anemone-like polyp with two rings of tentacles to capture food

Sea flowers

This sea fir (hydroid) looks a bit like a flowering plant, but it belongs to the same group of animals as corals, jellyfish, and sea anemonies. Sea firs grow fixed to surfaces, such as rocks and seaweeds, with branching colonies of anemone-like polyps. These have tentacles that are used to capture food particles carried past in the current. If disturbed, the sea fir will withdraw its polyps into its horny skeleton.

Sea mat growing on surface

The coral kingdom

In the clear, warm waters of the tropics, coral reefs cover vast areas. Most stony corals are colonies of many tiny, anemone-like polyps. Each polyp makes a hard limestone cup (skeleton) that protects its soft body. They do this with the help of microscopic, single-celled algae that live inside them. The algae need sunlight to grow, so coral reefs are found only in sunny, surface waters. Only the upper layer of a reef is made of living corals, which build upon skeletons of dead polyps. It is also home to soft corals and sea fans, which do not have stony skeletons.

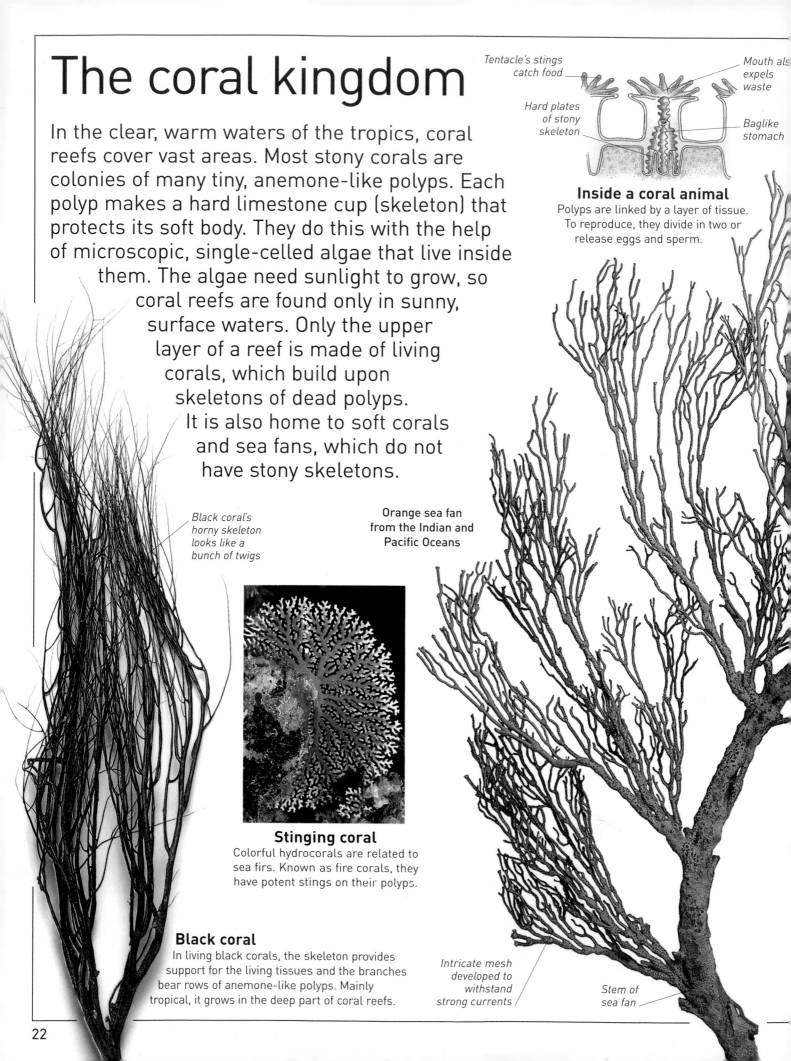

Tentacle's stings catch food

Hard plates of stony skeleton

Mouth also expels waste

Baglike stomach

Inside a coral animal
Polyps are linked by a layer of tissue. To reproduce, they divide in two or release eggs and sperm.

Black coral's horny skeleton looks like a bunch of twigs

Orange sea fan from the Indian and Pacific Oceans

Stinging coral
Colorful hydrocorals are related to sea firs. Known as fire corals, they have potent stings on their polyps.

Black coral
In living black corals, the skeleton provides support for the living tissues and the branches bear rows of anemone-like polyps. Mainly tropical, it grows in the deep part of coral reefs.

Intricate mesh developed to withstand strong currents

Stem of sea fan

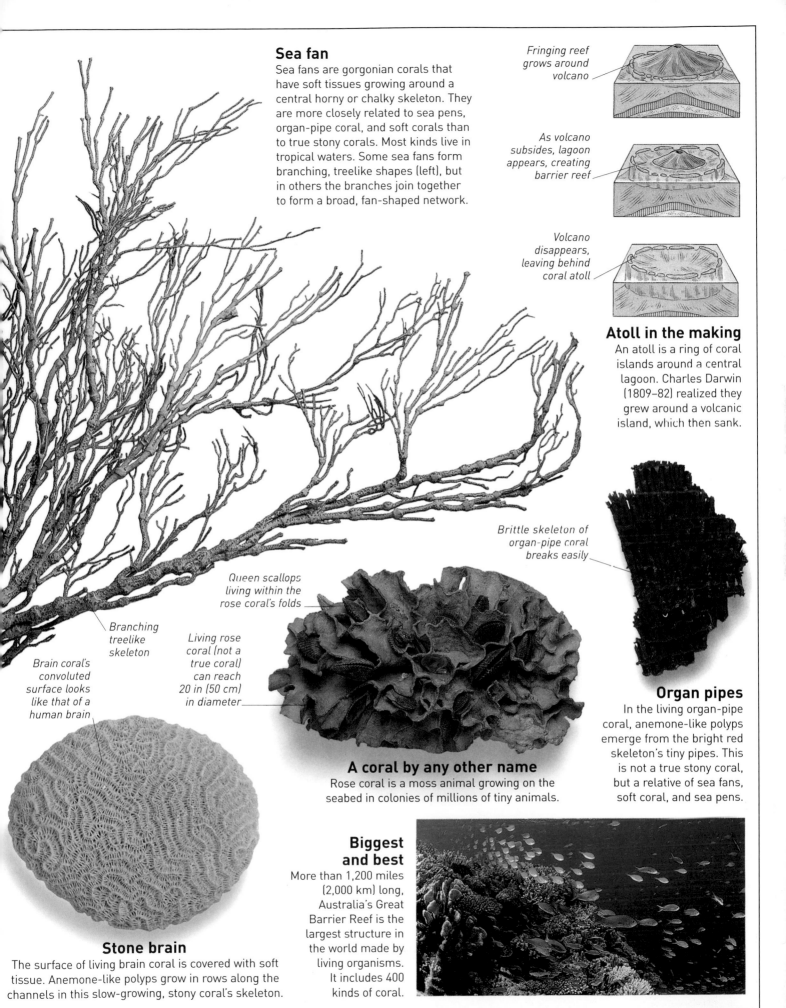

Sea fan

Sea fans are gorgonian corals that have soft tissues growing around a central horny or chalky skeleton. They are more closely related to sea pens, organ-pipe coral, and soft corals than to true stony corals. Most kinds live in tropical waters. Some sea fans form branching, treelike shapes (left), but in others the branches join together to form a broad, fan-shaped network.

Fringing reef grows around volcano

As volcano subsides, lagoon appears, creating barrier reef

Volcano disappears, leaving behind coral atoll

Atoll in the making

An atoll is a ring of coral islands around a central lagoon. Charles Darwin (1809–82) realized they grew around a volcanic island, which then sank.

Brittle skeleton of organ-pipe coral breaks easily

Branching treelike skeleton

Queen scallops living within the rose coral's folds

Living rose coral (not a true coral) can reach 20 in (50 cm) in diameter

Brain coral's convoluted surface looks like that of a human brain

Organ pipes

In the living organ-pipe coral, anemone-like polyps emerge from the bright red skeleton's tiny pipes. This is not a true stony coral, but a relative of sea fans, soft coral, and sea pens.

A coral by any other name

Rose coral is a moss animal growing on the seabed in colonies of millions of tiny animals.

Stone brain

The surface of living brain coral is covered with soft tissue. Anemone-like polyps grow in rows along the channels in this slow-growing, stony coral's skeleton.

Biggest and best

More than 1,200 miles (2,000 km) long, Australia's Great Barrier Reef is the largest structure in the world made by living organisms. It includes 400 kinds of coral.

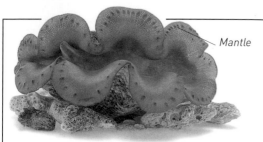

Mantle

A giant clam

The giant blue clam grows to about 12 in (30 cm) long. A horde of single-celled algae in its brightly colored mantle uses energy from sunlight to make their own food. The clam absorbs nutrients from the algae.

Life on a coral reef

Coral reefs support an amazing variety of marine life. Every bit of space provides shelter for some animal or plant. At night, a host of creatures emerges from coral caves and crevices to feed. All these living organisms depend on the stony corals that recycle scarce nutrients from the clear, blue, tropical waters. People, as well as animals, rely on coral reefs because they protect coastlines, and some island peoples live on coral atolls. Sadly, coral reefs are under threat, damaged by snorkelers and divers stepping on them, dynamited by fishermen, and polluted by sewage and oil spills.

Green color helps camouflage sea slug among seaweeds

Tentacles of sea anemone covered with stings to put off predators

The clown fish's slimy coat does not trigger the anemone's stings

Large eye for keeping a watch for danger

Side fin used to steer and change direction

Frilly lettuce

Sea slugs are related to sea snails but do not have shells. Many feed on the coral but the lettuce slug feeds on algae growing on the reef, by sucking the sap from their cells. Stored in the slug's digestive system, chloroplasts, the green part of plant cells, continue to trap energy from sunlight to make food.

Stripes break up clown fish's outline, making it more difficult for predators to see the fish on the reef

Living in harmony

Clown fish shelter in anemones living on coral reefs in the Pacific and Indian oceans. Unlike other fish, clown fish do not trigger the stings of their anemone home, because chemicals taken from the anemone are carried in the clown fish's slimy coat. Certain kinds of clown fish live only with certain kinds of anemone.

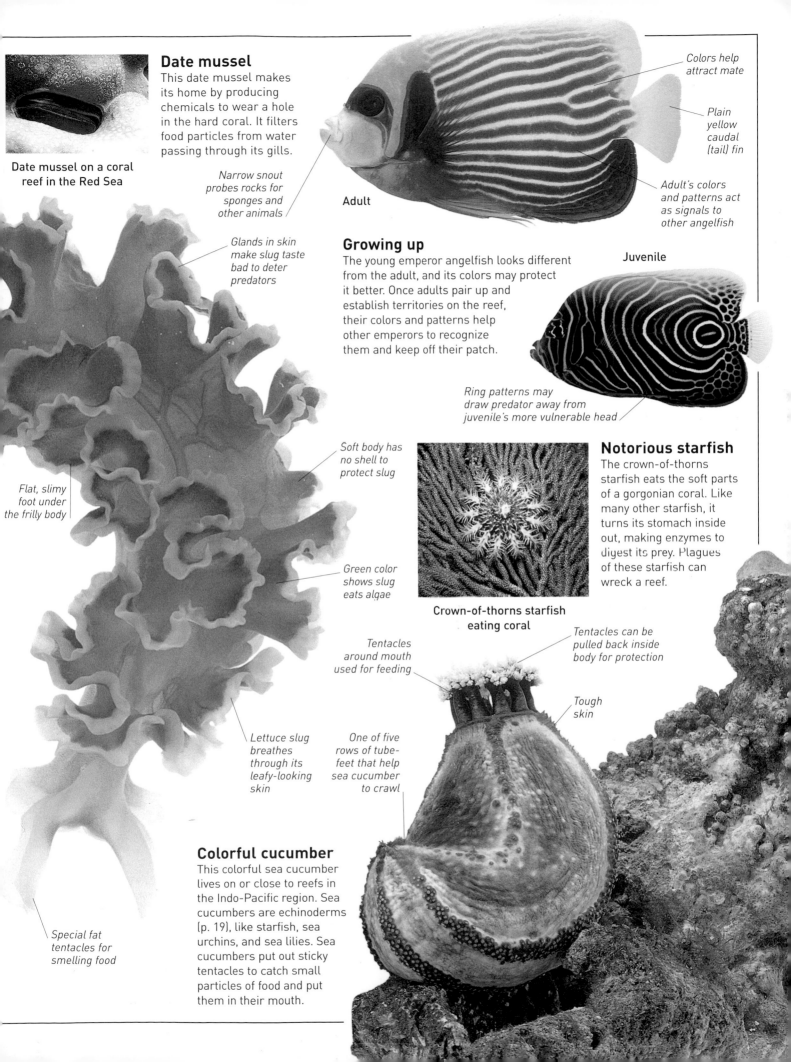

Date mussel
This date mussel makes its home by producing chemicals to wear a hole in the hard coral. It filters food particles from water passing through its gills.

Date mussel on a coral reef in the Red Sea

Narrow snout probes rocks for sponges and other animals

Colors help attract mate

Plain yellow caudal (tail) fin

Adult's colors and patterns act as signals to other angelfish

Adult

Glands in skin make slug taste bad to deter predators

Growing up
The young emperor angelfish looks different from the adult, and its colors may protect it better. Once adults pair up and establish territories on the reef, their colors and patterns help other emperors to recognize them and keep off their patch.

Juvenile

Ring patterns may draw predator away from juvenile's more vulnerable head

Soft body has no shell to protect slug

Notorious starfish
The crown-of-thorns starfish eats the soft parts of a gorgonian coral. Like many other starfish, it turns its stomach inside out, making enzymes to digest its prey. Plagues of these starfish can wreck a reef.

Crown-of-thorns starfish eating coral

Flat, slimy foot under the frilly body

Green color shows slug eats algae

Tentacles can be pulled back inside body for protection

Tentacles around mouth used for feeding

Tough skin

Lettuce slug breathes through its leafy-looking skin

One of five rows of tube-feet that help sea cucumber to crawl

Special fat tentacles for smelling food

Colorful cucumber
This colorful sea cucumber lives on or close to reefs in the Indo-Pacific region. Sea cucumbers are echinoderms (p. 19), like starfish, sea urchins, and sea lilies. Sea cucumbers put out sticky tentacles to catch small particles of food and put them in their mouth.

Sea meadows

The most abundant plants in the ocean are minute floating plants called phytoplankton. Like all plants, they need sunlight to grow, so they live in the ocean's upper zone. Light is most abundant in the tropics but nutrients are in short supply here. Huge phytoplankton blooms are found in cooler waters where nutrients (dead plant and animal waste) are brought up from the bottom during storms, and in both cool and warm waters where there are upwellings of nutrient-rich water. Phytoplankton are mostly eaten by tiny animals (zooplankton), which are eaten by small fish, which in turn are eaten by larger predators; some of the biggest fish and whales feed directly on zooplankton.

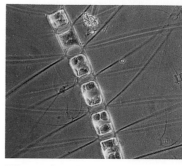

Plant food
This diatom is one of many phyto-plankton that drift in the ocean. Many diatoms are single cells, but this one consists of a chain of cells.

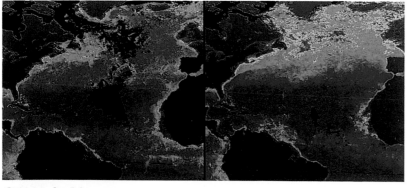

Glass jar to collect plankton sample

Plankton enters net at wide end

Older stage crab larva showing pincers

In the net
Scientists use special nets to study plankton. Commercial fishing relies on how much plankton there is for young fish to eat. Phytoplankton also help regulate our climate because they use so much carbon dioxide—one of the gases responsible for global warming.

Very fine mesh net traps tiny plants and animals drifting in the ocean

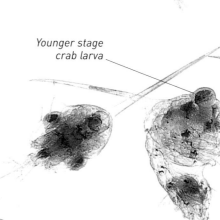

Younger stage crab larva

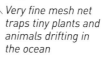

Ocean in bloom
Two images from a space satellite show phytoplankton densities in the Atlantic Ocean. Red shows where phytoplankton is densest through yellow, green, blue to violet where it is least dense. Phytoplankton's spring bloom (right) occurs when days are longer and more nutrients come up from the bottom. A second, smaller bloom of phytoplankton occurs in the fall.

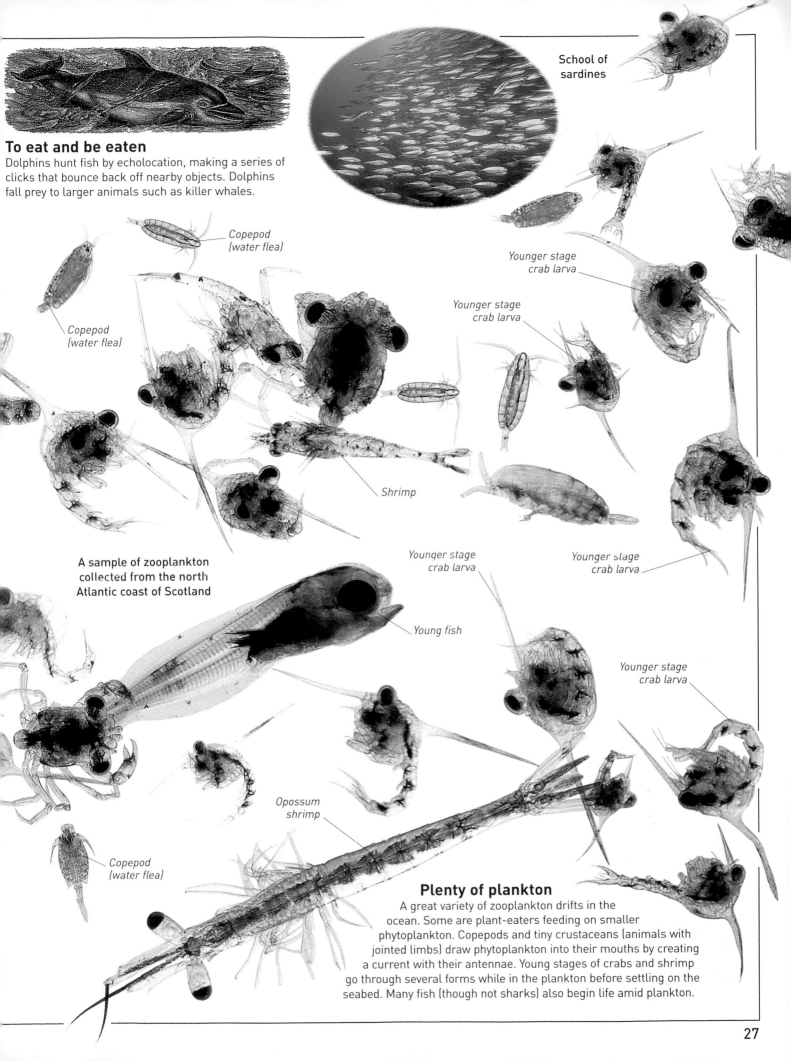

To eat and be eaten

Dolphins hunt fish by echolocation, making a series of clicks that bounce back off nearby objects. Dolphins fall prey to larger animals such as killer whales.

School of sardines

Copepod (water flea)

Copepod (water flea)

Younger stage crab larva

Younger stage crab larva

Shrimp

A sample of zooplankton collected from the north Atlantic coast of Scotland

Younger stage crab larva

Younger stage crab larva

Younger stage crab larva

Young fish

Younger stage crab larva

Opossum shrimp

Copepod (water flea)

Plenty of plankton

A great variety of zooplankton drifts in the ocean. Some are plant-eaters feeding on smaller phytoplankton. Copepods and tiny crustaceans (animals with jointed limbs) draw phytoplankton into their mouths by creating a current with their antennae. Young stages of crabs and shrimp go through several forms while in the plankton before settling on the seabed. Many fish (though not sharks) also begin life amid plankton.

Predators

Some ocean animals are herbivores (plant-eaters), which feed on seaweeds or phytoplankton. There are also many carnivores (meat-eaters), large and small. Some are swift hunters; others set traps for their prey, waiting with snapping jaws or stinging tentacles. Many animals strain food out of the water, and seabirds dive for a beakful of prey. Omnivores eat both plants and animals.

Cooperative feeding
Humpback whales encircle a school of fish, gulp in water and food, then expel the water through sievelike baleen plates in their mouths.

Tiny prey caught in mucus

Caught by slime
Many jellyfish sting their prey, but the common jellyfish traps tiny plankton in mucus from its bell. Four arms collect the food-laden slime and tiny hairlike cilia channel it into the mouth.

Fang face
The wolf fish has strong, fanglike teeth that crunch through the hard shells of crabs, sea urchins, and mussels. As the front set is worn down each year, or broken, it is replaced by a new set growing behind.

Dorsal fin runs along entire length of body

Crooked, yellow fang-like teeth

Pectoral fin

Tough, wrinkled skin helps protect wolf fish living near the seabed

Spines to protect urchin

Grazing away

The European common sea urchin grazes on seaweeds and animals such as sea mats that grow on the surface of the seaweeds. It uses the rasping teeth on the underside of its shell. If too many sea urchins are collected for food or tourist souvenirs, a rocky reef can become overgrown by seaweed.

Pelican diving

Tube-feet used to walk slowly along the seabed

Sea urchin's mouth surrounded by five rasping teeth

Tiny teeth of a basking shark

Pouch-like beak

Feeding on fishes

Like all pelicans, the brown pelican has a big beak with a large pouch of skin to capture fish. Only brown pelicans dive far below the surface for their prey. When the pelican surfaces, it drains the water from its pouch and swallows the fish.

To bite or not to bite

A tiger shark's pointed, serrated teeth can pierce and slice through almost anything, from hard-shelled turtles to seals and seabirds. A basking shark's rows of tiny teeth are not used at all—it filters food from water with a strainer of gill rakers.

Tiger shark's tooth

Any undigested pieces of food are ejected through the mouth

Stinging tentacle

Tentacle traps

Flowerlike Dahlia anemones are deadly traps for shrimp and small fish that brush past the tentacles. Hundreds of nematocysts (stinging cells) fire their stings, and the tentacles pass the stricken prey to the mouth in the center—the entrance to the baglike stomach.

Suckerlike disk lets Dahlia anemone attach to any hard surface

Homes and hiding

Staying hidden is one of the best means of defense—if a predator can't see you, it is less likely to eat you! Many sea animals shelter among seaweeds, in rocky crevices, or under the sand. Camouflage matching the colors and the texture of the background also helps sea creatures remain undetected. The sargassum fish even looks like bits of seaweed. Hard shells provide protection from weak-jawed predators. Sea snails and clams make their own shells that cover the body, while crabs and lobsters have outer shells, like suits of armor, covering the body and each jointed limb.

What a weed

This fish lives among floating clumps of sargassum seaweed, where frilly growths on its head, body, and fins help it avoid being seen by predators, making a realistic disguise.

Blending in

Cuttlefish have different colored pigments and rapidly change color to escape predators. The brain signals tiny bags of pigment in its skin to contract, making the skin paler.

Cuttlefish becomes darker when pigment bags expand

Hermit crab leaving old whelk shell

Anemone

When out of its shell, crab is vulnerable to predators

Investigating its new home by checking size with its claws

Hermit crab moves into a perspex shell

All change

Hermit crabs lack armor around their abdomens, so they live in the empty shells of sea snails and other creatures. Like all crustaceans, a hermit crab grows by shedding its hard, outer skeleton and does this in the safety of its snail-shell home. As it grows larger, it looks for a larger snail shell to move into. When it finds one that is just right, it carefully pulls its body out of its old shell, tucking it quickly into the new one.

Leg with pointed claws to get a grip on seabed when walking

Antenna

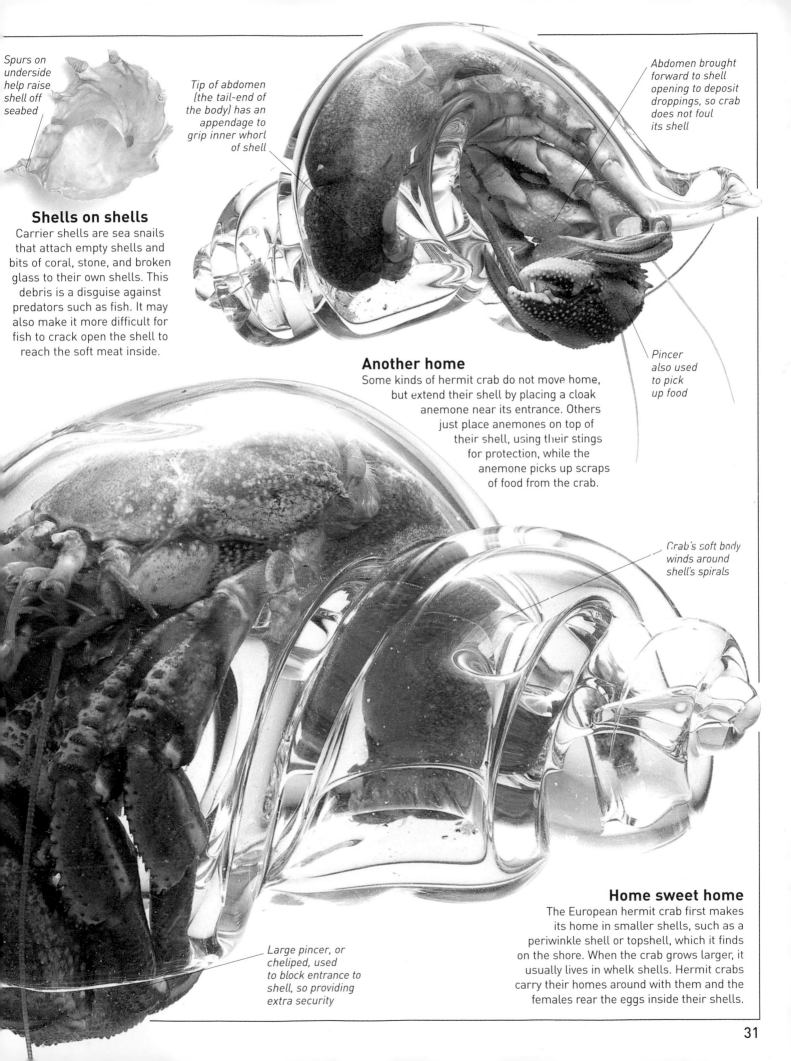

Spurs on underside help raise shell off seabed

Shells on shells

Carrier shells are sea snails that attach empty shells and bits of coral, stone, and broken glass to their own shells. This debris is a disguise against predators such as fish. It may also make it more difficult for fish to crack open the shell to reach the soft meat inside.

Tip of abdomen (the tail-end of the body) has an appendage to grip inner whorl of shell

Abdomen brought forward to shell opening to deposit droppings, so crab does not foul its shell

Pincer also used to pick up food

Another home

Some kinds of hermit crab do not move home, but extend their shell by placing a cloak anemone near its entrance. Others just place anemones on top of their shell, using their stings for protection, while the anemone picks up scraps of food from the crab.

Crab's soft body winds around shell's spirals

Large pincer, or cheliped, used to block entrance to shell, so providing extra security

Home sweet home

The European hermit crab first makes its home in smaller shells, such as a periwinkle shell or topshell, which it finds on the shore. When the crab grows larger, it usually lives in whelk shells. Hermit crabs carry their homes around with them and the females rear the eggs inside their shells.

Attack and defense

Many sea creatures have weapons to attack prey or defend themselves from predators. Some produce venom (poison) for defense and often warn of their danger with markings. The lionfish's stripes may alert enemies to its venomous spines, but being easy to see, they hunt at dusk when they can surprise their prey. Disappearing in a cloud of ink is a useful trick used by octopuses, squid, and cuttlefish. But no defense method is foolproof, since even the most venomous jellyfish can be eaten by carnivorous turtles that are immune to their stings.

Deadly stonefish
Never step on a stonefish. Sharp spines on its back inject a venom that causes such pain that the shock can kill.

Long, dorsal spine with venom glands in grooves

Ink cloud forming around cuttlefish

Ink screen
Cephalopods (squid, cuttlefish, and octopuses) produce a cloud of ink to confuse an enemy and allow time to flee. The ink is ejected in a jet of water from a tubelike funnel near the head.

Horny projection above eye

Maerl (a chalky, red seaweed) grows in a thick mass along the stony seabed

Three venomous anal spines

Blue for danger
If this octopus senses danger, blue-ringed spots appear on its skin, warning of its poisonous bite. Living in shallow, often tropical waters, this blue-ringed octopus is the size of your hand, but its bite can be fatal.

Keep clear
A predator trying to bite a striped lionfish may be impaled by one or more of its poisonous spines. If it survives, the predator will remember the stripes and the danger and leave lionfish alone in future. Found in tropical waters, lionfish can swim openly looking for smaller prey with little risk of attack.

Stripes warn predators that lionfish is dangerous

Two venomous spines on tail can pierce the swimmer's skin and inject its venom

Sting ray's sting is sharp and serrated, easily piercing the skin

Pectoral fin used for swimming

Sting in the tail

This blue-spotted ray lives in warm waters and is found lurking on the seabed. If stepped on, it injects venom that causes shooting pains in the foot that last over an hour.

Painting of sea monsters, c. 1880s

Something scary

Early sailors knew that some creatures of the deep were deadly. Tales about sea monsters were often greatly exaggerated. They were also made up to account for ships lost at sea.

Vicious jellyfish

Jellyfish are known for their stings, but the nastiest stings are those of the box jellyfish in the Pacific Ocean. The stings produce welts on anyone who comes in contact with the tentacles. A badly stung person can die quickly.

When shell is closed, there is still a gap between the shell's two halves

Tentacles always on show

Shaggy shells

These gaping file shells cannot pull their orange tentacles inside the two halves of their shell for protection, so the tentacles produce a sticky, sour-tasting substance to deter predators. Gaping file shells also put out byssus threads for anchorage. If dislodged, they can move by expelling water from their shells and using their tentacles like oars.

Shell is up to 1 in (2.5 cm) long

The jet set

One way to swim quickly and escape from predators is by jet propulsion. Some mollusks, such as clams, squid, and octopuses, do this by squirting water from the body cavity. Squid are best at this—their bodies are streamlined to reduce drag (resistance to water). Some kinds of scallop also use jet propulsion and are among the few clams that can swim. If attacked, the common octopus uses this same technique to jet off.

Tentacle tales
A Norwegian story tells of the Kraken, a sea monster that wrapped its giant arms around ships and sank them. The legend may be based on the mysterious giant squid that live in deep waters. Dead specimens have been found, but in 2004 a living one was finally photographed.

Jet propulsion
The engines powering a jet plane produce jets of air to fly. An octopus uses jets of water to dart through the ocean.

Flexible funnel
At the edge of the octopus's baglike body is a funnel. It can bend to aim the jet of water backward or forward.

Funnel

Long arms to grasp prey

Powerful suckers grip the rock, so octopus can pull itself along

1 On the bottom
The common octopus hides during the day in its rocky lair, coming out at night to look for such food as crustaceans.

Sucker is sensitive to touch and taste

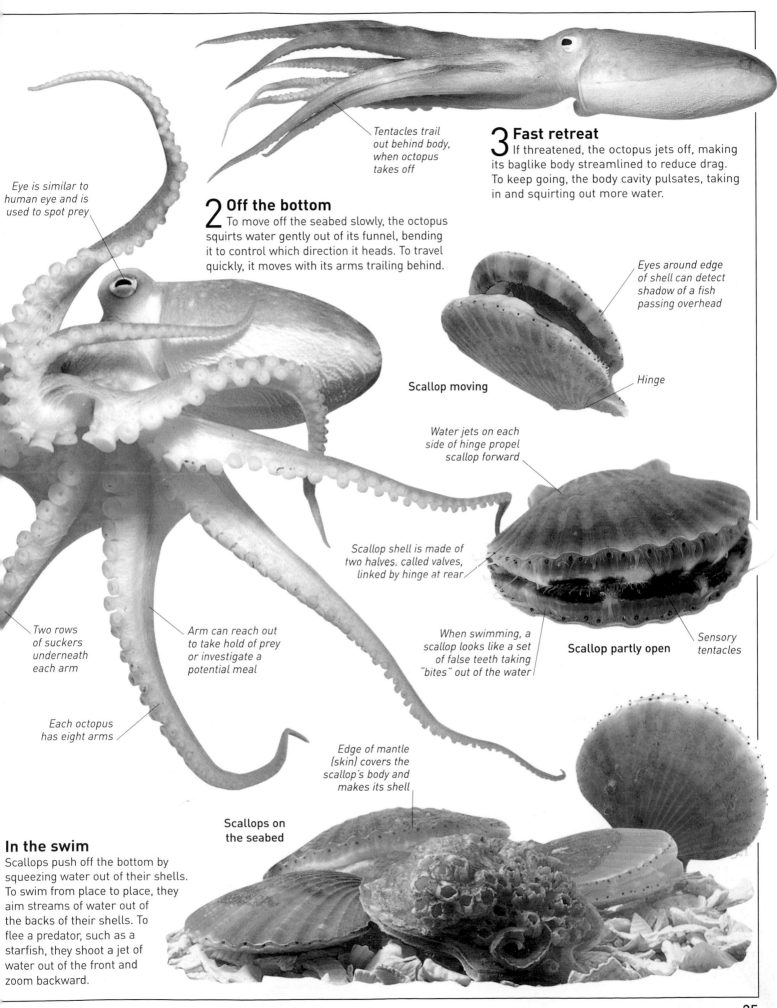

Tentacles trail out behind body, when octopus takes off

3 Fast retreat
If threatened, the octopus jets off, making its baglike body streamlined to reduce drag. To keep going, the body cavity pulsates, taking in and squirting out more water.

Eye is similar to human eye and is used to spot prey

2 Off the bottom
To move off the seabed slowly, the octopus squirts water gently out of its funnel, bending it to control which direction it heads. To travel quickly, it moves with its arms trailing behind.

Eyes around edge of shell can detect shadow of a fish passing overhead

Scallop moving

Hinge

Water jets on each side of hinge propel scallop forward

Two rows of suckers underneath each arm

Arm can reach out to take hold of prey or investigate a potential meal

Scallop shell is made of two halves, called valves, linked by hinge at rear

When swimming, a scallop looks like a set of false teeth taking "bites" out of the water

Scallop partly open

Sensory tentacles

Each octopus has eight arms

Edge of mantle (skin) covers the scallop's body and makes its shell

Scallops on the seabed

In the swim
Scallops push off the bottom by squeezing water out of their shells. To swim from place to place, they aim streams of water out of the backs of their shells. To flee a predator, such as a starfish, they shoot a jet of water out of the front and zoom backward.

Moving along

Seawater is much denser than air, making it harder to move through. To be a fast swimmer, it helps to have a shape that is streamlined like a torpedo to reduce drag (resistance to water). The density of seawater also helps to support an animal's body weight—the heaviest animal of all is the blue whale, which weighs up to 165 tons (150 metric tons). Some ocean animals get up enough speed underwater to leap briefly into the air, but not all are good swimmers. Many can only swim slowly, or drift in the currents, crawl along the bottom, or burrow in the sand. Others simply stay put, anchored to the seabed.

Flying fish

Flying fish gather speed, leap into the air, and spread their side fins to glide for more than 30 seconds.

At school

Fish often swim together in a school (like these blue-striped snappers). The moving mass of fish makes it harder for a predator to target one individual, plus there are more pairs of eyes to detect danger.

In the swing

During the day, many electric rays hide on the sandy seabed, relying on their electric organs for defense, although they swim if disturbed and at night they search for prey. There are about 20 members of the electric ray family, mostly living in warm waters. Most other rays have spindly tails (unlike the electric ray's broad tail), and move through water using their pectoral fins.

Electric ray's smooth skin can be either blackish or red-brown in color

Water enters through spiracle and is pumped out through gill slits underneath

Some electric rays grow to 6 ft (1.8 m) and weigh up to 110 lb (50 kg)

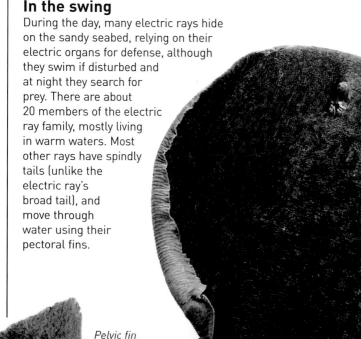

Pelvic fin

Swimming sequence of an electric ray

Diving deep

True seals use front flippers to steer, and move by beating their back flippers and tails from side to side. Harbor seals (right) can dive to 300 ft (90 m), but the elephant seal dives to over 5,000 ft (1,500 m). Underwater, seals close their nostrils to stop water from entering the airways and use oxygen stored in the blood.

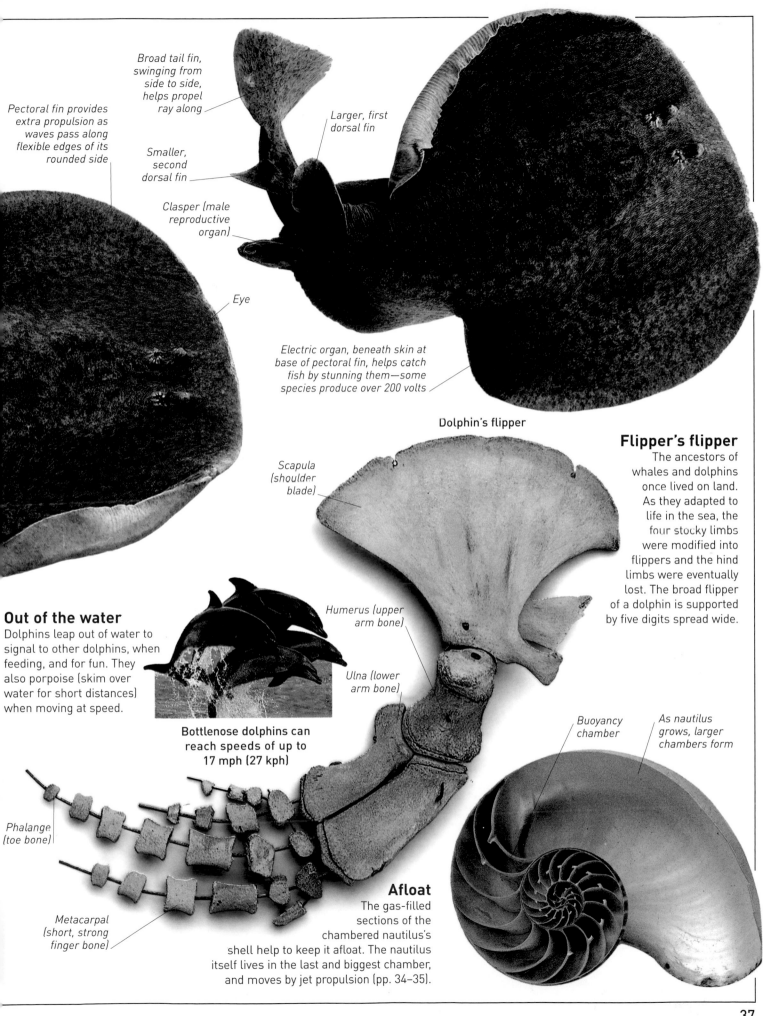

Broad tail fin, swinging from side to side, helps propel ray along

Larger, first dorsal fin

Pectoral fin provides extra propulsion as waves pass along flexible edges of its rounded side

Smaller, second dorsal fin

Clasper (male reproductive organ)

Eye

Electric organ, beneath skin at base of pectoral fin, helps catch fish by stunning them—some species produce over 200 volts

Dolphin's flipper

Scapula (shoulder blade)

Flipper's flipper

The ancestors of whales and dolphins once lived on land. As they adapted to life in the sea, the four stocky limbs were modified into flippers and the hind limbs were eventually lost. The broad flipper of a dolphin is supported by five digits spread wide.

Humerus (upper arm bone)

Ulna (lower arm bone)

Out of the water

Dolphins leap out of water to signal to other dolphins, when feeding, and for fun. They also porpoise (skim over water for short distances) when moving at speed.

Bottlenose dolphins can reach speeds of up to 17 mph (27 kph)

Buoyancy chamber

As nautilus grows, larger chambers form

Phalange (toe bone)

Metacarpal (short, strong finger bone)

Afloat

The gas-filled sections of the chambered nautilus's shell help to keep it afloat. The nautilus itself lives in the last and biggest chamber, and moves by jet propulsion (pp. 34–35).

Ocean travelers

Some sea animals travel great distances to find the best places to feed and breed. Whales feed in the cold, food-rich waters of the far north or south, then travel to the warm waters of the tropics to breed. Turtles, seals, and seabirds feed out at sea, but come ashore to reproduce. Salmon grow in the ocean and return to rivers to breed. Ocean currents help to speed animals on their way. Even animals that cannot swim can hitch a ride on another animal or drift on a piece of wood.

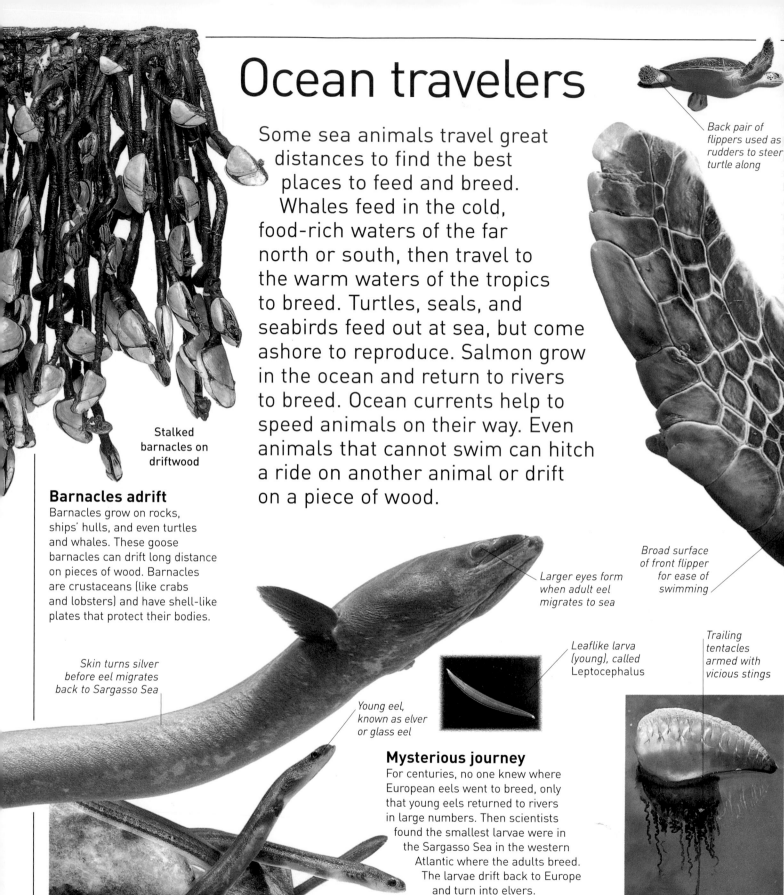

Back pair of flippers used as rudders to steer turtle along

Stalked barnacles on driftwood

Barnacles adrift
Barnacles grow on rocks, ships' hulls, and even turtles and whales. These goose barnacles can drift long distance on pieces of wood. Barnacles are crustaceans (like crabs and lobsters) and have shell-like plates that protect their bodies.

Skin turns silver before eel migrates back to Sargasso Sea

Larger eyes form when adult eel migrates to sea

Broad surface of front flipper for ease of swimming

Leaflike larva (young), called Leptocephalus

Trailing tentacles armed with vicious stings

Young eel, known as elver or glass eel

Mysterious journey
For centuries, no one knew where European eels went to breed, only that young eels returned to rivers in large numbers. Then scientists found the smallest larvae were in the Sargasso Sea in the western Atlantic where the adults breed. The larvae drift back to Europe and turn into elvers.

Portuguese man-of-war
Not a true jellyfish but a siphonophore (a relative of sea firs), the man-of-war has a gas-filled float that keeps it at the surface where it is blown by the wind and drifts with the currents.

Swimming sequence of a green turtle

Turtle shell is streamlined for gliding through water

Underwater flier

Green turtles live in warm waters in the Atlantic, Pacific, and Indian oceans. Like all turtles, they come ashore to lay their eggs. First, the females mate in shallow water with the waiting males. Later, at night, the females crawl up the beach to lay their eggs in the sand before returning to the water. Some travel hundreds of miles to the beach where they themselves hatched.

Front pair of flippers help turtle to "fly" through water

Turtles are air breathers so must come to the surface to breathe through their nostrils

Green turtle (*Chelonia mydas*) is endangered

Turtle trip

In Japanese legend, Urashima Taro rides into the ocean on a turtle. After some time, he yearns for home. The sea goddess gives him a box that he must never open. Back home, he finds everything has changed and no one knows him. He opens the box and breaks the spell, turning into a very old man because he has spent 300 years at sea.

The twilight zone

Between the sunlit waters of the upper ocean and the black depths is the twilight zone, around 650–3,300 ft (200–1,000 m) below the surface. Fish living here often have rows of light organs on their bellies to help camouflage them against the little light that filters down from above. Many animals shelter in the twilight zone by day, hiding from daytime hunters such as seabirds, and then swim upward to feed in the food-rich surface water at night. Others spend most of their lives here, eating any available food.

Hunter of the depths
Viper fish have an impressive set of long, daggerlike teeth to grab their fish prey, which they attract with a lure dangling from the front of the dorsal fin. To swallow prey, such as a hatchet fish (above left), the hinged jaws open very wide.

Fin ray

Jumbo squid can reach 12 ft (3.6 m) to tips of tentacles

Sail-like dorsal fin can be raised and lowered

A giant of a squid
The Atlantic giant squid can weigh as much as one ton. Suckers on the tentacles cling onto prey, and sperm whales often bear the scars of an attack.

Dorsal fin can be used for herding fish prey

Mythical merman
Strange creatures lurk in the depths, but nothing like this.

Large gill flap

Model of a lancet fish

Pointed teeth for grabbing fish

Pectoral fin

Long and skinny
The lancet fish has a narrow body, lightweight bones, and little muscle. It catches squid and other fish living at the same depths.

Pelvic fin

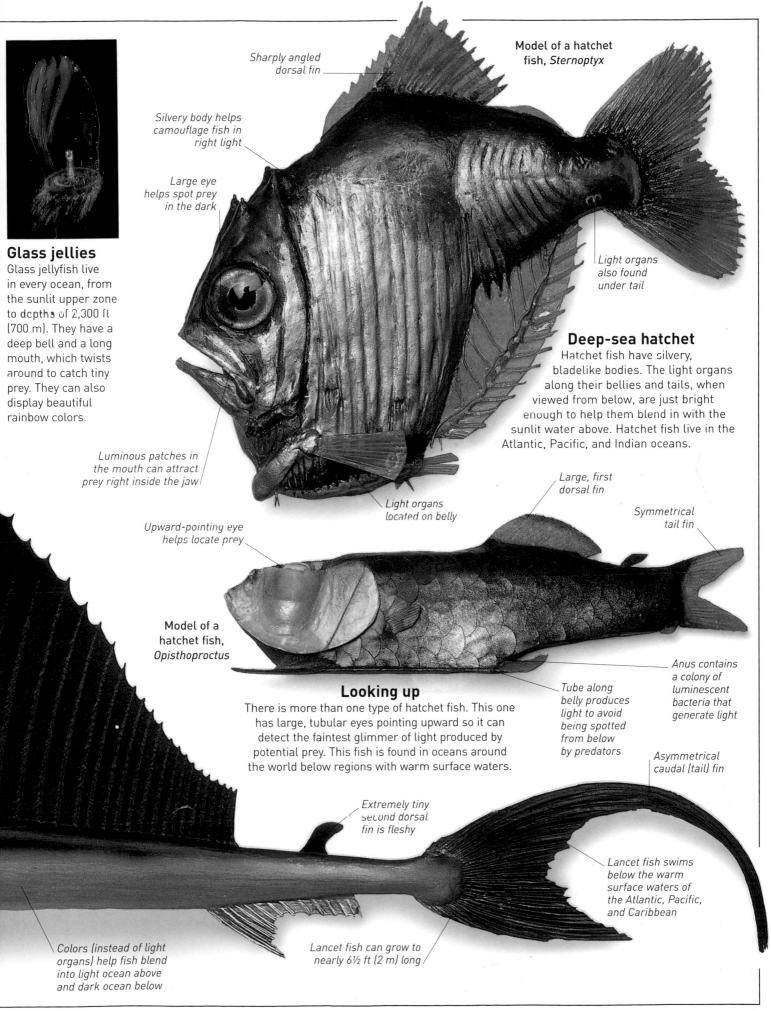

Model of a hatchet fish, *Sternoptyx*

Sharply angled dorsal fin

Silvery body helps camouflage fish in right light

Large eye helps spot prey in the dark

Glass jellies
Glass jellyfish live in every ocean, from the sunlit upper zone to depths of 2,300 ft (700 m). They have a deep bell and a long mouth, which twists around to catch tiny prey. They can also display beautiful rainbow colors.

Luminous patches in the mouth can attract prey right inside the jaw

Light organs also found under tail

Deep-sea hatchet
Hatchet fish have silvery, bladelike bodies. The light organs along their bellies and tails, when viewed from below, are just bright enough to help them blend in with the sunlit water above. Hatchet fish live in the Atlantic, Pacific, and Indian oceans.

Upward-pointing eye helps locate prey

Light organs located on belly

Large, first dorsal fin

Symmetrical tail fin

Model of a hatchet fish, *Opisthoproctus*

Looking up
There is more than one type of hatchet fish. This one has large, tubular eyes pointing upward so it can detect the faintest glimmer of light produced by potential prey. This fish is found in oceans around the world below regions with warm surface waters.

Tube along belly produces light to avoid being spotted from below by predators

Anus contains a colony of luminescent bacteria that generate light

Asymmetrical caudal (tail) fin

Extremely tiny second dorsal fin is fleshy

Lancet fish swims below the warm surface waters of the Atlantic, Pacific, and Caribbean

Colors (instead of light organs) help fish blend into light ocean above and dark ocean below

Lancet fish can grow to nearly 6½ ft (2 m) long

The darkest depths

There is no light in the oceans below 3,300 ft (1,000 m), just blackness. Many fish in the dark zone are black, too, and almost invisible. Light organs are used as signals to find a mate or to lure prey. Food is scarce in the cold, dark depths so most deep-sea animals are small. Fish with huge mouths and stretchy stomachs make the most of what little food rains down from above.

Lateral line organs sense vibrations in water made by moving prey

Umbrella mouth gulper

The gulper eel swims along slowly with its huge mouth wide open, ready to swallow any food it finds, such as shrimp and small fish. The adults live in the lower part of the twilight zone and in the dark zone. The leaflike larvae are found in the sunlit zone from 300–650 ft (100–200 m). As they grow, the young gulper eels descend into deeper water.

Adults grow to about 30 in (75 cm) from the tips of their long tails to their heads

Gulper eel lives in the dark depths below temperate and tropical surface waters

Long lower jaw

Tiny eye on end of nose

Fishing line

The whipnose has a long, whiplike lure for attracting passing prey. The prey approaches, mistaking the lure for food, and is then snapped up.

Whipnose grows to 5 in (13 cm) in length

Monster movies

Movies often feature scary sea monsters. So much of the deep ocean is unexplored that there could be strange animals yet to be discovered—they would most likely be small, since there is so little food at these depths.

Model of a whipnose, which lives in the Atlantic and Pacific oceans

Lower lobe of tail fin is longer than upper lobe

Binocular eyes

Gigantura's extraordinary tubular eyes are probably used to pinpoint the glowing light organs of its prey. Its skin can stretch so that it can swallow fish larger than itself.

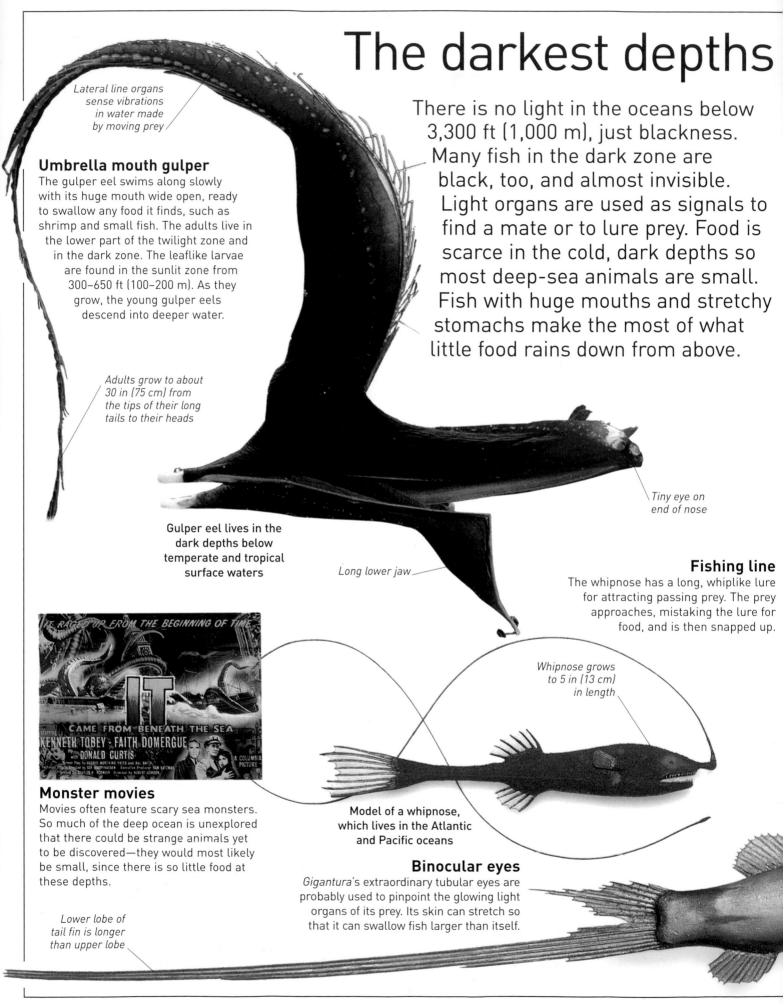

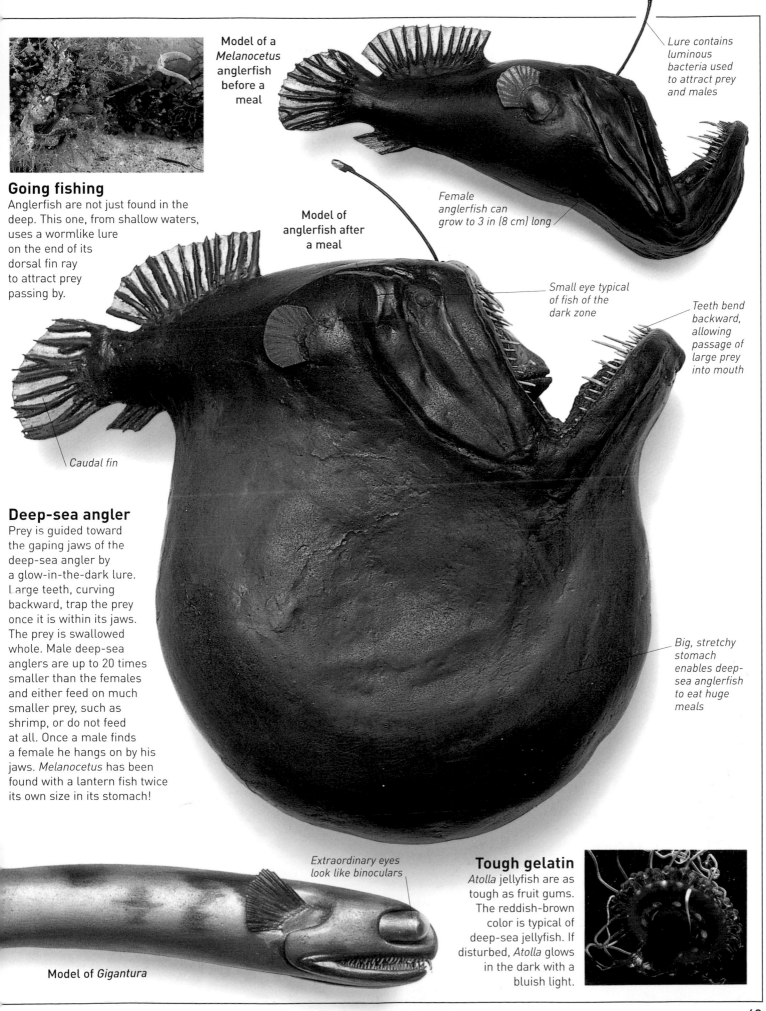

Model of a *Melanocetus* anglerfish before a meal

Lure contains luminous bacteria used to attract prey and males

Female anglerfish can grow to 3 in (8 cm) long

Going fishing
Anglerfish are not just found in the deep. This one, from shallow waters, uses a wormlike lure on the end of its dorsal fin ray to attract prey passing by.

Model of anglerfish after a meal

Small eye typical of fish of the dark zone

Teeth bend backward, allowing passage of large prey into mouth

Caudal fin

Deep-sea angler
Prey is guided toward the gaping jaws of the deep-sea angler by a glow-in-the-dark lure. Large teeth, curving backward, trap the prey once it is within its jaws. The prey is swallowed whole. Male deep-sea anglers are up to 20 times smaller than the females and either feed on much smaller prey, such as shrimp, or do not feed at all. Once a male finds a female he hangs on by his jaws. *Melanocetus* has been found with a lantern fish twice its own size in its stomach!

Big, stretchy stomach enables deep-sea anglerfish to eat huge meals

Extraordinary eyes look like binoculars

Model of *Gigantura*

Tough gelatin
Atolla jellyfish are as tough as fruit gums. The reddish-brown color is typical of deep-sea jellyfish. If disturbed, *Atolla* glows in the dark with a bluish light.

On the bottom

The bottom of the deep ocean is not an easy place to live. There is little food, and it is dark and cold. Much of the seabed is covered with soft clays or mudlike oozes made of skeletons of tiny sea animals and plants. Some animals feed on the seabed, extracting small food particles from the ooze. While others filter nutrients from the water. These tiny food particles are the remains of dead animals (and their droppings) and plants that have sunk down from above. Because food is scarce and temperatures so low, most animals living in the deep ocean take a long time to grow.

Telegraph cables being laid along the bottom of the Atlantic Ocean, c. 1870

Dried remains of sea anemones

Glass-rope sponge

This cup-shaped sponge grows anchored to the soft seabed by its long stem of glassy, needlelike strands. Sea anemones often grow on the stem.

Stem formed by long, glassy spikes made of silica

Not a true spider

Sea spiders belong to a group called pycnogonids. Some deep-sea spiders have a leg span of 24 in (60 cm) across, and can stride along without stirring up clouds of particles.

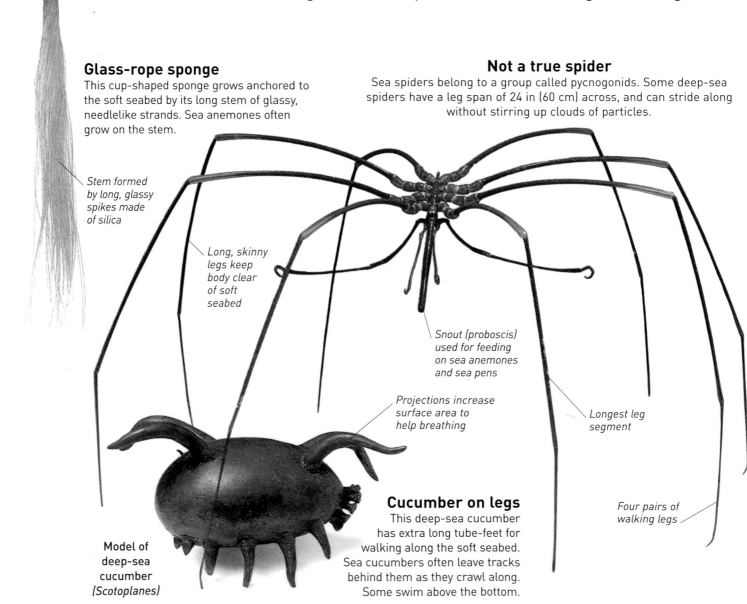

Long, skinny legs keep body clear of soft seabed

Snout (proboscis) used for feeding on sea anemones and sea pens

Projections increase surface area to help breathing

Longest leg segment

Cucumber on legs

This deep-sea cucumber has extra long tube-feet for walking along the soft seabed. Sea cucumbers often leave tracks behind them as they crawl along. Some swim above the bottom.

Four pairs of walking legs

Model of deep-sea cucumber (*Scotoplanes*)

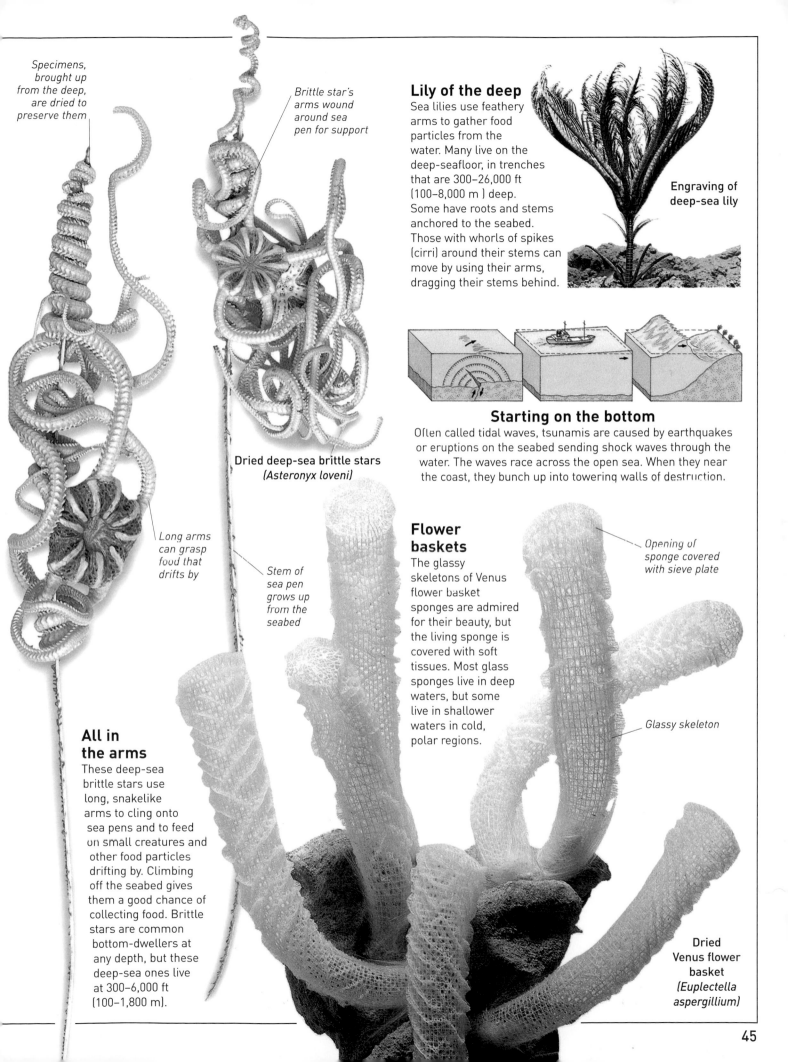

Specimens, brought up from the deep, are dried to preserve them

Brittle star's arms wound around sea pen for support

Dried deep-sea brittle stars
(Asteronyx loveni)

Long arms can grasp food that drifts by

Stem of sea pen grows up from the seabed

Lily of the deep
Sea lilies use feathery arms to gather food particles from the water. Many live on the deep-seafloor, in trenches that are 300–26,000 ft (100–8,000 m) deep. Some have roots and stems anchored to the seabed. Those with whorls of spikes (cirri) around their stems can move by using their arms, dragging their stems behind.

Engraving of deep-sea lily

Starting on the bottom
Often called tidal waves, tsunamis are caused by earthquakes or eruptions on the seabed sending shock waves through the water. The waves race across the open sea. When they near the coast, they bunch up into towering walls of destruction.

Flower baskets
The glassy skeletons of Venus flower basket sponges are admired for their beauty, but the living sponge is covered with soft tissues. Most glass sponges live in deep waters, but some live in shallower waters in cold, polar regions.

Opening of sponge covered with sieve plate

Glassy skeleton

All in the arms
These deep-sea brittle stars use long, snakelike arms to cling onto sea pens and to feed on small creatures and other food particles drifting by. Climbing off the seabed gives them a good chance of collecting food. Brittle stars are common bottom-dwellers at any depth, but these deep-sea ones live at 300–6,000 ft (100–1,800 m).

Dried Venus flower basket
(Euplectella aspergillium)

Deep heat

In parts of the ocean floor, very hot, mineral-rich water gushes out. These vents, or hot springs, exist where the gigantic plates that make up the Earth's crust are moving apart. Cold seawater sinks deep into cracks where the water is heated. At temperatures of up to 750°F (400°C), hot water spews out, carrying minerals that form chimneys (black smokers). The hot water helps bacteria to grow, which create food from the hydrogen sulfide in the water. These microbes support an extraordinary community of animals.

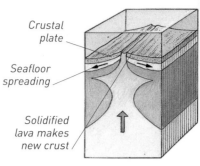

Crustal plate

Seafloor spreading

Solidified lava makes new crust

Growing ocean
New areas of ocean floor are created at spreading centers between two tectonic plates. When hot, molten rock (lava) emerges from within the crust, the lava cools and hardens, adding material to the edge of both plates. Old areas of ocean floor are destroyed when one plate slides under another.

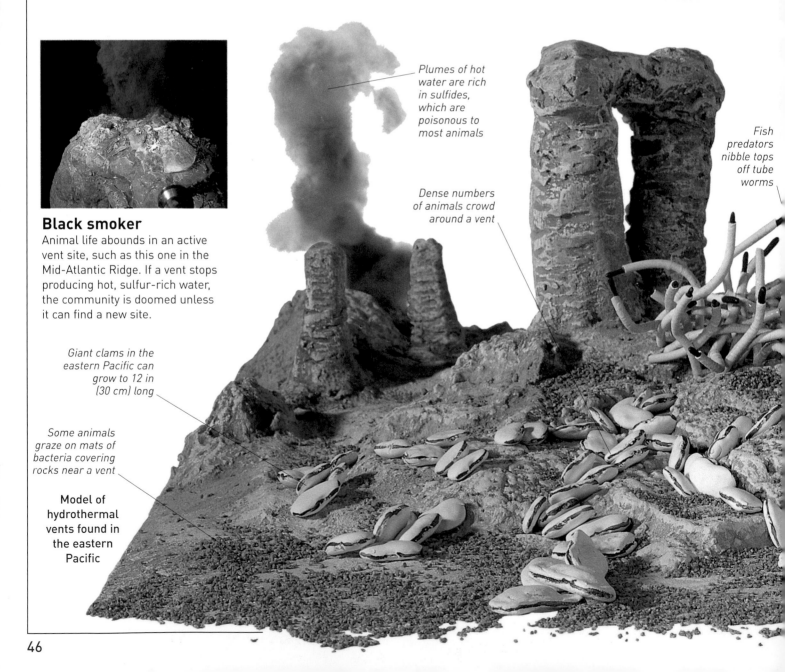

Black smoker
Animal life abounds in an active vent site, such as this one in the Mid-Atlantic Ridge. If a vent stops producing hot, sulfur-rich water, the community is doomed unless it can find a new site.

Plumes of hot water are rich in sulfides, which are poisonous to most animals

Dense numbers of animals crowd around a vent

Fish predators nibble tops off tube worms

Giant clams in the eastern Pacific can grow to 12 in (30 cm) long

Some animals graze on mats of bacteria covering rocks near a vent

Model of hydrothermal vents found in the eastern Pacific

Black smoker chimney can reach 30 ft (10 m) high

Chimney made from mineral deposits

Deep-sea fish photographed from Alvin near a vent on the Mid-Atlantic Ridge

Alvin by the support ship, *Atlantis II*

Pioneering submersible

The US submersible, *Alvin*, was the first to take scientists down to observe marine life near the Galapagos vents in the east Pacific in the 1970s. Since then, *Alvin* has made many dives to vents around the world to depths of 12,500 ft (3,800 m).

Vent communities

Vent communities vary. This model shows black smokers in the eastern Pacific, where giant clams and tube worms are the most distinctive animals—as are hairy snails in the Mariana Trench and eyeless shrimp along the Mid-Atlantic Ridge.

Tube worm can grow to 10 ft (3 m) long

Giant tube worm has bacteria inside its body that provide it with food

Diverse divers

People have always wanted to explore the ocean, to find wrecks and treasure, study marine life, and (in modern times) drill for oil and gas. The first diving gear was a simple bell containing air. Later, diving suits with hard helmets enabled divers to go deeper and stay longer, with air pumped down a line. In the 1940s, the aqualung or SCUBA (Self-Contained Underwater Breathing Apparatus) enabled divers to carry their air supply in tanks on their backs.

Umbilical supplies air and electricity for light

Weight belt

Underwater worker
This diver, wearing a wetsuit for warmth, gets air into the helmet via a line to the surface. A harness around the diver's waist carries tools.

Rope connecting bell to surface

Wooden bell

Weight

Early diving bell
In 1690, Edmund Halley's diving bell allowed divers to be resupplied with barrels of air that were lowered from the surface and linked to the bell and the divers by a tube. The bell, open at the bottom, was used at depths of 60 ft (18 m).

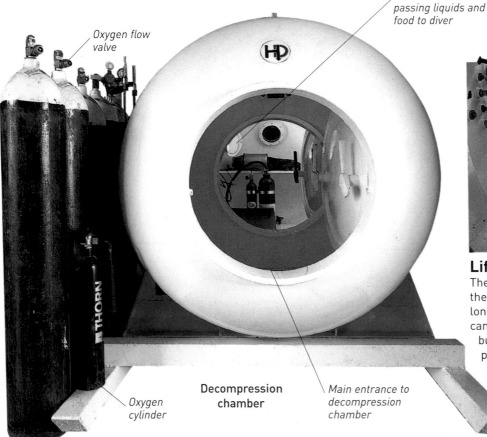

Oxygen flow valve

"Medical lock" for passing liquids and food to diver

Decompression chamber

Oxygen cylinder

Main entrance to decompression chamber

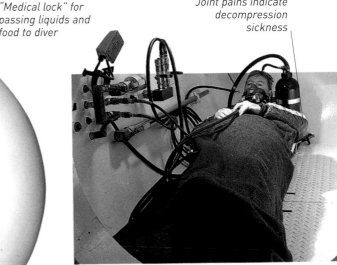

Joint pains indicate decompression sickness

Lifesaver
The weight of water increases the pressure on the body. If a diver comes up too quickly after a long or deep dive, the sudden drop in pressure can cause the nitrogen in the air supply to form bubbles in the diver's blood and tissues. This painful, sometimes fatal condition is called decompression sickness (the bends). A decompression chamber raises the pressure to move the bubbles out through the lungs, then slowly lowers it to the normal level at the surface.

An early
diving
suit

A classic diving suit

The "Standard" diving suit was invented by Augustus Siebe in the 1830s. Modified versions of this hard-helmeted suit are still in use today. The tunic made of layers of canvas and rubber is waterproof. The copper and brass helmet fits onto a heavy breastplate (corselet) that is bolted onto the tunic. Wearing heavy boots and two extra weights, the diver would sink to depths of about 200 ft (60 m).

Helmet equipped with two-way communication system so diver can talk to someone on the surface

Weight is about 30 lb (13 kg)

Diver has two weights—one at the front, a second at the back

Helmet made of copper and brass

Face plate

Wrench for tightening bolts on breastplate

Breastplate screwed to tunic using six, eight, or 12 bolts

Complete "Standard" diving suit

Long johns made from wool for greater warmth and insulation

Rubber cuff for extra waterproofing

Suit made of a layer of rubber between two layers of canvas

Ribbed cuff helps trap warm air

Each boot weighs 18 lb (8 kg)

Leather boot with lead base to help weigh diver down in water

Submarines

The first submarines were simple machines that could travel a short distance underwater and were useful in warfare. Later versions were powered by diesel or gas while on the surface and by batteries underwater. Since 1955, nuclear power has allowed submarines to travel great distances before refueling. Today, they are equipped with sonar and computer systems to navigate, track other vessels, and launch missiles.

Snort mast renews and expels air with help of bellows

Delayed action mine

Augur drills into enemy ship to attach mine

Vertical propeller

Side propeller powered by foot pedals

External steering bar operated by diver

"Turtle" hero

A one-man wooden submarine, the *Turtle*, was used during the American Revolutionary War in 1776 to try to attach a mine to an English ship that was blockading New York Harbor. The operator became disorientated by carbon dioxide building up inside the *Turtle* and jettisoned the bomb.

Underwater adventure

Inspired by the invention of modern submarines, this 1900 engraving depicted a scene in the year 2000 with people enjoying a journey in a submarine liner. Tourists can now take trips in small submarines to view marine life in places such as the Red Sea. However, most people explore the underwater world by learning to SCUBA dive or snorkel.

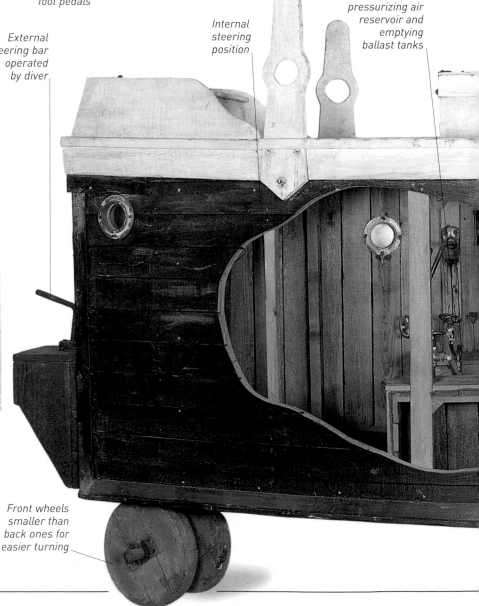

Internal steering position

Hand pump for pressurizing air reservoir and emptying ballast tanks

Front wheels smaller than back ones for easier turning

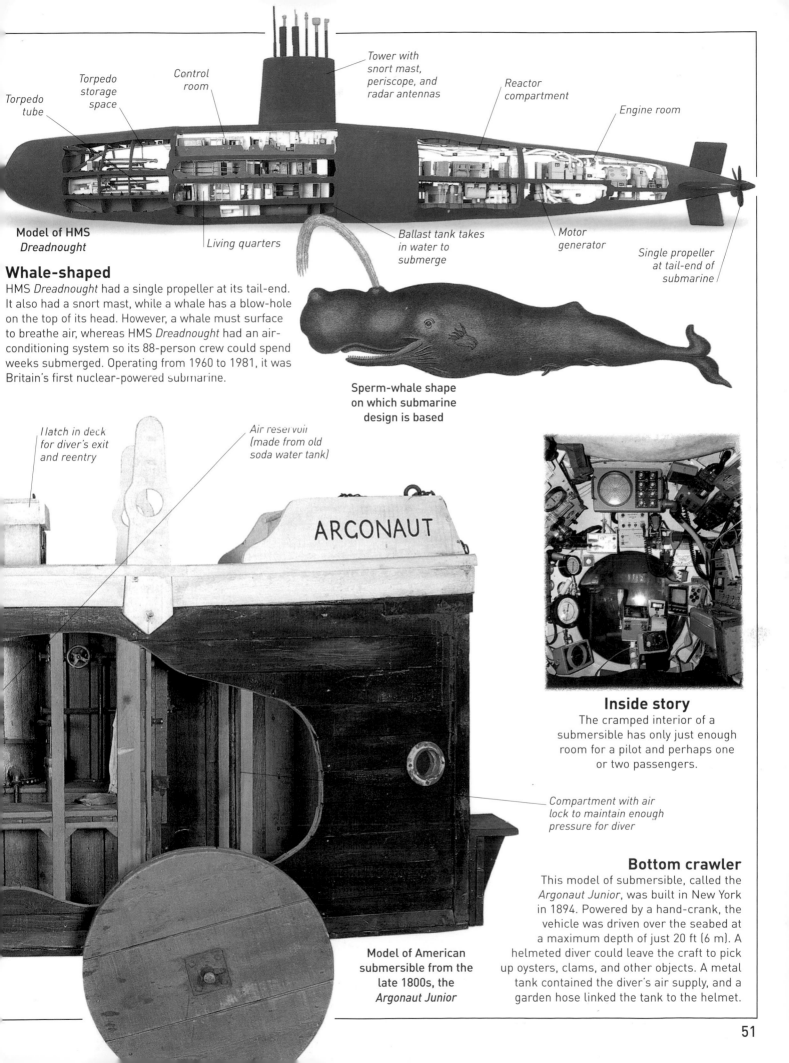

Torpedo tube

Torpedo storage space

Control room

Tower with snort mast, periscope, and radar antennas

Reactor compartment

Engine room

Model of HMS *Dreadnought*

Living quarters

Ballast tank takes in water to submerge

Motor generator

Single propeller at tail-end of submarine

Whale-shaped

HMS *Dreadnought* had a single propeller at its tail-end. It also had a snort mast, while a whale has a blow-hole on the top of its head. However, a whale must surface to breathe air, whereas HMS *Dreadnought* had an air-conditioning system so its 88-person crew could spend weeks submerged. Operating from 1960 to 1981, it was Britain's first nuclear-powered submarine.

Sperm-whale shape on which submarine design is based

Hatch in deck for diver's exit and reentry

Air reservoir (made from old soda water tank)

ARGONAUT

Inside story
The cramped interior of a submersible has only just enough room for a pilot and perhaps one or two passengers.

Compartment with air lock to maintain enough pressure for diver

Bottom crawler
This model of submersible, called the *Argonaut Junior*, was built in New York in 1894. Powered by a hand-crank, the vehicle was driven over the seabed at a maximum depth of just 20 ft (6 m). A helmeted diver could leave the craft to pick up oysters, clams, and other objects. A metal tank contained the diver's air supply, and a garden hose linked the tank to the helmet.

Model of American submersible from the late 1800s, the *Argonaut Junior*

Ocean explorers

Image from 1900 of a submarine bus in 2000

The ocean has always been a place of mystery, with little to see on the surface. The first depth soundings were made by dropping a lead weight on a line until the operator felt it hit the bottom. Echo sounders, invented during World War I, bounced pulses of sound off the seabed. This led to sonar systems that could map the ocean floor. For centuries, the only clues to deep-sea life were creatures brought up in fishermen's nets or washed ashore. In the 1870s, HMS *Challenger*'s trawls showed that the deep ocean did contain life. Today, manned and unmanned submersibles reach otherwise inaccessible waters. Even so, much of the ocean is yet to be explored.

Glorious GLORIA

GLORIA, for Geological Long Range Inclined Asdic (sonar), was used to survey the ocean floor. Covering 7,700 sq miles (20,000 sq km) in a day, GLORIA scanned more than five percent of the world's oceans in 20 years.

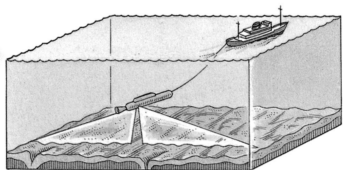

Gloria at work

To survey the seabed, GLORIA was towed behind its mother ship at a speed of 10 knots. Sound pulses from GLORIA would span across the seabed for up to 18 miles (30 km) on each side. GLORIA picked up echoes bouncing back from features on the seabed. These were processed by onboard computers to produce maps of the seafloor.

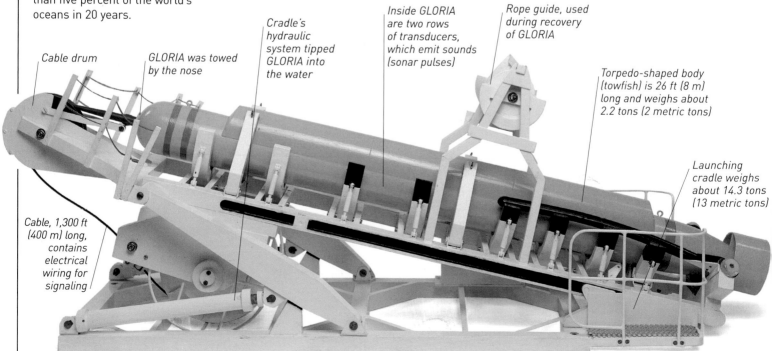

Cradle's hydraulic system tipped GLORIA into the water

Inside GLORIA are two rows of transducers, which emit sounds (sonar pulses)

Rope guide, used during recovery of GLORIA

Cable drum

GLORIA was towed by the nose

Torpedo-shaped body (towfish) is 26 ft (8 m) long and weighs about 2.2 tons (2 metric tons)

Launching cradle weighs about 14.3 tons (13 metric tons)

Cable, 1,300 ft (400 m) long, contains electrical wiring for signaling

Snorkeling

A simple way to observe life underwater is to snorkel just below the surface. The swimmer breathes through a snorkel that sticks out above water.

Air expelled through end of snorkel

Fins propel swimmer along, but arms should be kept near the body for streamlining

Scuba diver looking at grouper fish in the Red Sea

Face mask traps air to let swimmer view life in the water

Swimmer breathes in air and expels it through mouthpiece

Snorkel tube

SCUBA diving

SCUBA equipment has proved invaluable in the study of marine life in shallow waters. Instead of bringing animals into an aquarium, marine biologists can observe them in the wild.

Deep stars

Many submersibles have been used for underwater exploration. The deepest dive ever was to 35,800 ft (10,912 m) in the Mariana Trench in 1960.

Deep Star can reach depths of 4,000 ft (1,200 m)

Fins used in snorkeling and SCUBA diving

Autosub

This Autonomous Underwater Vehicle (AUV) can explore remote parts of the ocean. AUVs are unmanned and operate without being tethered to a ship or submersible.

Autosub uses a suite of sensors to collect data

Mechanical arm used to lower Autosub into the water

Wrecks on the seabed

Ever since people took to the sea in boats, there have been wrecks on the seabed. Mud and sand cover wooden hulls, protecting the timbers by keeping out the oxygen that speeds up decay. Metal-hulled ships are badly corroded by seawater; the *Titanic*'s steel hull could disintegrate within a hundred years. Wrecks in shallow water get covered by plant and animal life, turning them into living reefs. Uncovering wrecks and their objects can tell us much about life in the past.

Less valuable silver coin

Glittering gold
Spanish coins, much in demand by pirates, sometimes ended up on the seabed when a ship sank.

Sonar equipment

Titanium sphere

IFRE
DCN C

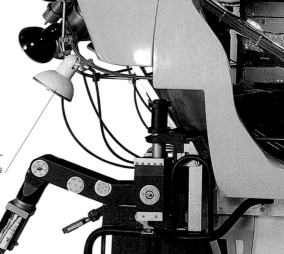

Super sub
The French submersible, *Nautile*, recovered objects from the seabed surrounding the wreck of the *Titanic*. Only a submersible could dive deep enough to reach the wreck, 2.5 miles (3,780 m) down. The *Nautile* takes about 90 minutes to reach the site, and it can stay down for eight hours. The pilot, copilot, and observer sit in a small sphere made of titanium metal, which protects them from the huge pressure at these depths.

Valuable property
In 1892, divers worked on the wreck of the tug *L'Abeille*, off Le Havre, France, to bring up salvage (items of value).

Lights for video camera

Manipulator arm for picking objects off seabed

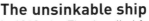

Sad reminders
Many items recovered from the *Titanic* wreck were not valuable, but everyday items such as this flatware remind us of those who used them before they died.

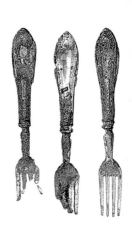

The unsinkable ship
In 1912, the *Titanic* sailed from England to New York City on its maiden voyage. When it hit an iceberg, it took 2 hours and 40 minutes to sink, with only 705 people saved out of 2,228. The wreck was found in 1985 by a French-US team using remote-controlled video equipment on an unmanned probe.

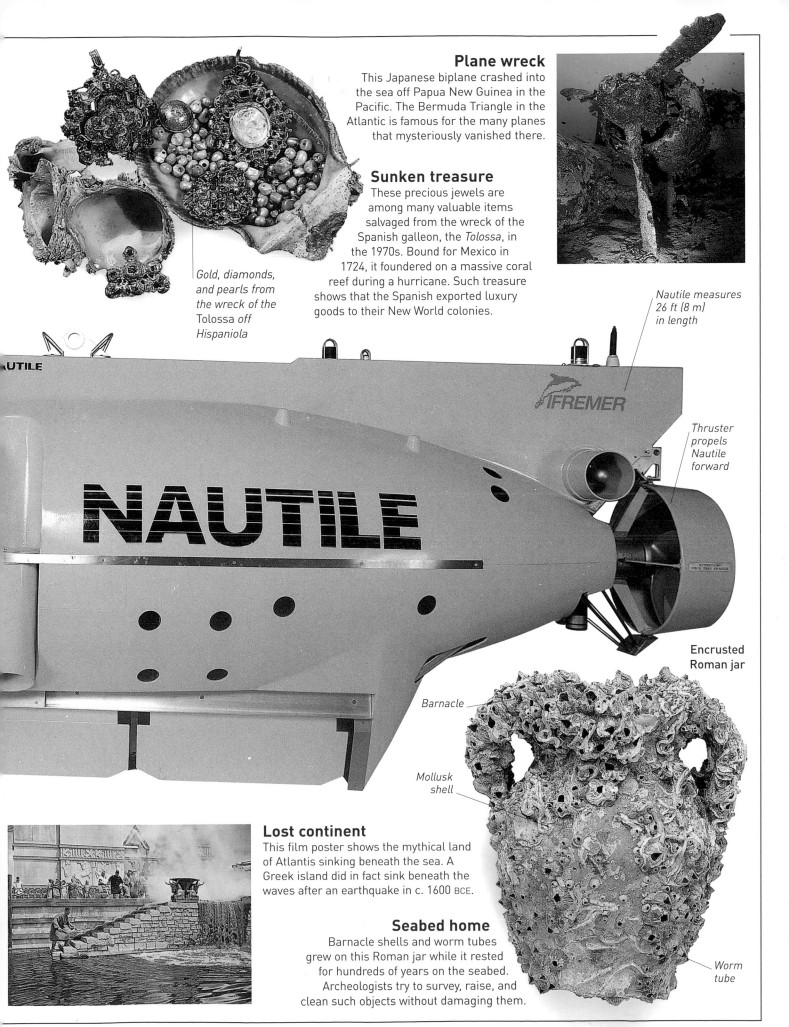

Plane wreck
This Japanese biplane crashed into the sea off Papua New Guinea in the Pacific. The Bermuda Triangle in the Atlantic is famous for the many planes that mysteriously vanished there.

Sunken treasure
These precious jewels are among many valuable items salvaged from the wreck of the Spanish galleon, the *Tolossa*, in the 1970s. Bound for Mexico in 1724, it foundered on a massive coral reef during a hurricane. Such treasure shows that the Spanish exported luxury goods to their New World colonies.

Gold, diamonds, and pearls from the wreck of the Tolossa *off Hispaniola*

Nautile measures 26 ft (8 m) in length

Thruster propels Nautile forward

NAUTILE

Encrusted Roman jar

Barnacle

Mollusk shell

Lost continent
This film poster shows the mythical land of Atlantis sinking beneath the sea. A Greek island did in fact sink beneath the waves after an earthquake in c. 1600 BCE.

Seabed home
Barnacle shells and worm tubes grew on this Roman jar while it rested for hundreds of years on the seabed. Archeologists try to survey, raise, and clean such objects without damaging them.

Worm tube

Harvesting fish

More than 100 million tons of fish are caught around the world each year. Some fish are caught by hand-thrown nets and traps in local waters, but far more are caught at sea by fishing vessels using the latest technology. Some fish are caught on long lines with many hooks, or ensnared when they swim into long walls of drift nets. With sonar able to detect schools of fish, there are few places where fish can escape notice, even at 3,300 ft (1,000 m). If too many fish are caught, however, stocks take a long time to recover.

1 Hatching
Salmon begin life in rivers and streams. The fry (alevins) hatch from eggs laid in a shallow hollow among gravel and feed on the egg sac.

2 Young salmon
At a few weeks old, the egg sac disappears, so young salmon must feed on tiny insects in the river. The young salmon (called parr) stay in the river for a year or more, before turning into silvery smolt, which head for the sea.

3 At sea
Atlantic salmon spend up to four years at sea, feeding on other fish and putting on several pounds annually. Then the mature salmon return to the home rivers and streams where they hatched. They recognize their home stream by a number of clues, including the water's "smell."

Fin rays are well-developed

Large, first dorsal fin

Pelvic fin

Pectoral fin

Operculum (flap covering gills)

Teeth for gripping slippery prey

Fish farming
To meet the demand for fish, young salmon are reared in freshwater and then released into pens in calm seawaters, such as sea lochs. To help them grow quickly, they are fed with dried fish pellets. However, parasites called sea lice, common among farmed salmon, are infecting and killing wild salmon.

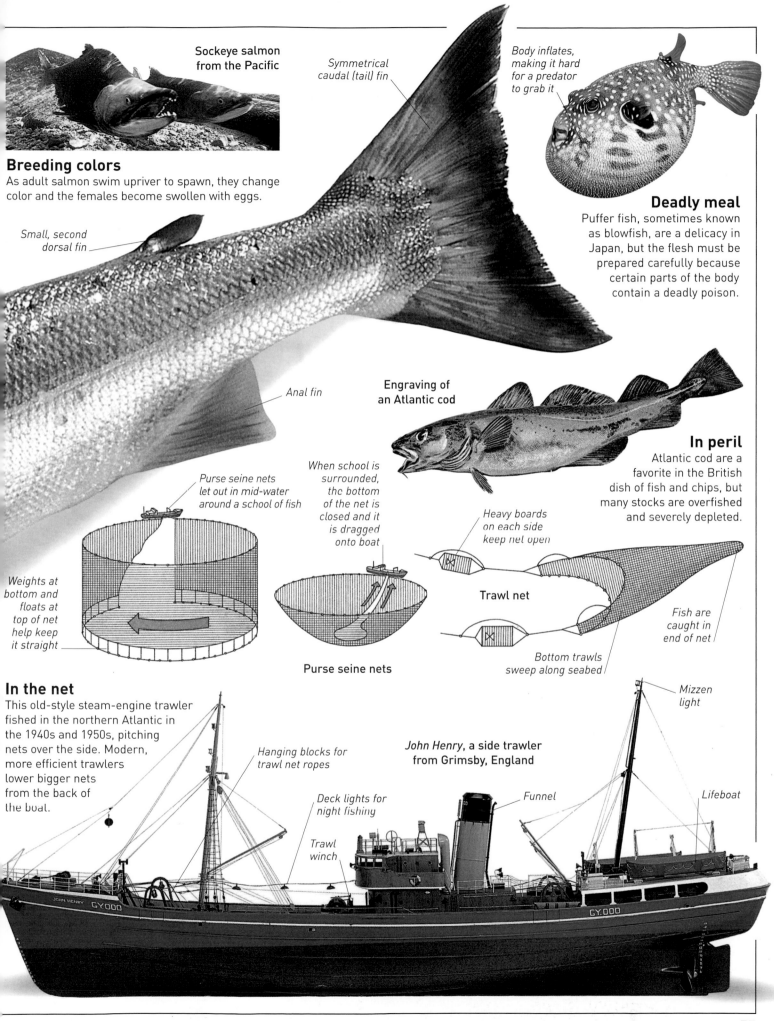

Sockeye salmon from the Pacific

Breeding colors
As adult salmon swim upriver to spawn, they change color and the females become swollen with eggs.

Small, second dorsal fin

Symmetrical caudal (tail) fin

Body inflates, making it hard for a predator to grab it

Deadly meal
Puffer fish, sometimes known as blowfish, are a delicacy in Japan, but the flesh must be prepared carefully because certain parts of the body contain a deadly poison.

Anal fin

Engraving of an Atlantic cod

In peril
Atlantic cod are a favorite in the British dish of fish and chips, but many stocks are overfished and severely depleted.

Purse seine nets let out in mid-water around a school of fish

When school is surrounded, the bottom of the net is closed and it is dragged onto boat

Heavy boards on each side keep net open

Trawl net

Fish are caught in end of net

Weights at bottom and floats at top of net help keep it straight

Purse seine nets

Bottom trawls sweep along seabed

In the net
This old-style steam-engine trawler fished in the northern Atlantic in the 1940s and 1950s, pitching nets over the side. Modern, more efficient trawlers lower bigger nets from the back of the boat.

Hanging blocks for trawl net ropes

John Henry, a side trawler from Grimsby, England

Mizzen light

Deck lights for night fishing

Funnel

Lifeboat

Trawl winch

JOHN HENRY GY.000

GY.000

Ocean products

People have always harvested plants and animals from the ocean, from fish, crustaceans (shrimp, lobster), and mollusks (clams, squid) to sea cucumbers and seaweeds. Most are collected for food, although some sea animals and seaweeds are now cultivated to meet demand for products and to prevent overcollecting the ocean's wildlife. Some sea creatures are made into amazing products, however, many (such as mother-of-pearl buttons) are now replaced by synthetic materials.

Yarn dyed purple from pigment of sea snails

Royal purple
Sea snails were used to make a purple dye for clothes worn by kings in ancient times. The liquid was extracted from huge quantities of salted snails left in vats gouged out of rocks, then heated to concentrate the dye.

Slate-pencil sea urchin from tropical coral reefs in the Indo-Pacific

Short, blunt spines surround mouth

Long, very strong spines help protect urchin from predators

Five, strong white teeth protrude from urchin's mouth (viewed from underneath)

Soft skeleton left after processing living sponge

Useful spines
The spines of this sea urchin were once used as pencils to write on slate boards. Slate-pencil urchins are still collected, with their spines made into wind chimes. Urchins use their big spines to help them walk across the seabed when they leave their crevices to feed at night.

Spines help urchin move and to hold it in place

Soft skeleton
Bath sponges grow among sea grasses in reef lagoons. When brought up from the sandy seabed, the sponges are covered with slimy, living tissues. Natural sponges are prone to diseases and are overcollected.

Seaweed farm
In Japan, seaweed is used in crackers and to wrap raw fish packages. Red seaweed is grown on bamboo poles, collected, and dried. The seaweed's gelatinlike agar is used in foods and in medical research. Seaweed is also made into fertilizer.

Shiny pearls

Pearls are produced by mussels and oysters in response to irritation. Natural pearls form around a piece of grit that gets between the oyster's shell and its skin (mantle). Tissues from the mantle surround the grit and produce mother-of-pearl layers. Pearls are cultivated by inserting particles into a clam.

Double strand of blue pearls

Shell can close to protect itself from predators

Salt pans

When seawater evaporates, a salt-crystal crust is left behind. Large quantities of sea salt are produced by flooding shallow ponds (pans) with seawater and letting the water evaporate in the hot sun. Sea salt is produced in places with warm weather and little rain.

Gloves can be made from byssus threads of noble pen shell

Tapered shell is brittle

Noble pen shell grows to 24 in (60 cm) in length

Silver cross inlaid with abalone shell

Hole to expel water and waste

Byssus threads made by shell to anchor it to seabed

Golden threads

In the Mediterranean, the pen shell produces a thick mat of byssus threads. These threads were once collected, spun into fine, golden thread, and then woven into cloth. Perhaps this cloth started the ancient Greek legend of the golden fleece.

Rainbow hues

Inside an abalone shell are all the colors of the rainbow. The heavy shell's mother-of-pearl is used to make jewelry and buttons. These shells are popular with New Zealand's Maoris. Abalones are also eaten.

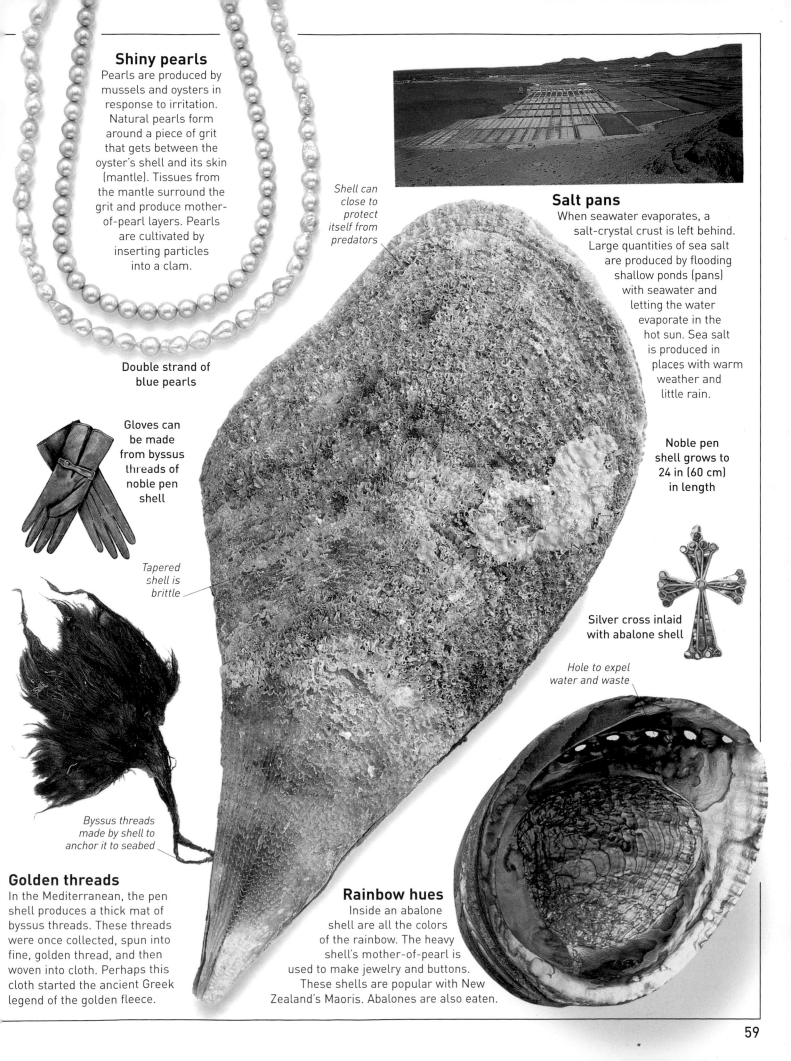

Oil and gas

Valuable reservoirs of oil and gas lie hidden beneath the seabed. Only certain kinds of rock hold oil and gas, but must be in shallow enough water to be reached by drilling. Geologists find the reservoirs by sending shock waves through the seabed and using the returning signals to distinguish between the rock layers. Temporary rigs are set up to see if the oil is of the right quality and quantity. To extract oil or gas, the rig is replaced by a more permanent oil platform, which is firmly anchored to the seabed. Oil can be piped ashore or stored on floating vessels (FPSOs) until it is loaded onto tankers.

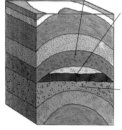

Impermeable rock stops oil from moving up

Oil is trapped in porous, reservoir rock

Porous rock lets oil pass through

Death and decay
Plant and bacteria remains fell to the ancient seabed and were covered by layers of mud. Heat and pressure turned them into oil, then gas, which rises.

Wind turbines
Oil reservoirs run dry, but wind turbines are a source of renewable energy. This wind farm operates off North Wales, UK.

Tallest structure on this platform is flare stack for safety reasons

At work
Platform workers check the drill bit that is used to cut through the rock. Special mud is sent down pipes to cool the bit, wash out the ground-up rock, and prevent the oil from gushing out.

On fire
Oil and gas are highly flammable. Accidents such as the North Sea's *Piper Alpha* disaster in 1988, in which 167 people died, have led to improved safety measures.

Floating production
Floating vessels called FPSOs (Floating Production, Storage, Offloading) store the oil and gas produced from nearby drilling platforms and undersea wells until it is taken away by tankers. FPSOs work well in deep-water locations that are too far to connect to the shore by seabed pipelines. They can also move out of the way of hurricanes or drifting icebergs.

FPSO GIRASSOL

Newt suit

A thick-walled suit resists pressure. When underwater, the diver breathes air at normal pressure as if inside a submersible. This allows a diver to go deeper without having to undergo decompression (p. 48). Newt suits (left) are used in oil exploration to depths of 1,200 ft (365 m).

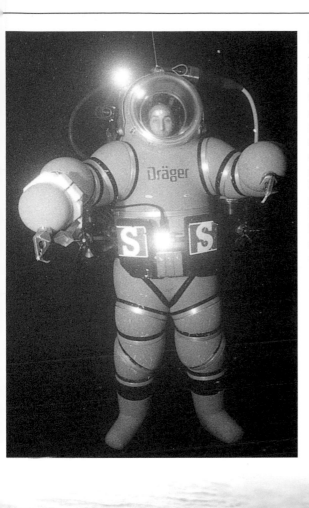

Airlifted

Helicopters deliver crew and supplies to oil platforms far out at sea. Up to 400 people can live and work on an oil platform, including geologists, cooks, and the mechanics who look after the machinery.

On the bottom

Divers (minus Newt suits), doing repairs underwater, work longer if they return to a pressurized chamber, then back into the sea, without having to decompress after each dive.

Helicopter pad—fresh food and milk are flown in

Living quarters

Fireproof lifeboat gives better chance of survival

Strong structure to withstand buffeting by wind and waves

Jewelry made of teeth of great white shark, now vulnerable

Oceans in peril

Oceans and ocean life are under threat. Overharvesting has depleted many ocean animals, from whales to fish, while sewage and industrial waste are dumped into the sea, carrying chemicals that disrupt the food chain. Oil spills smother and poison marine life. Nets and garbage dumped at sea can choke turtles or trap birds. Today, laws help to stop ocean pollution and protect marine life.

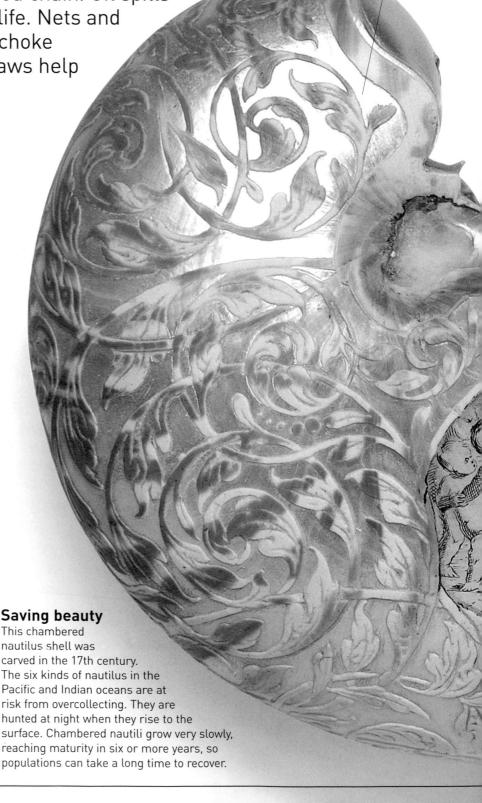

Cut to show mother-of-pearl

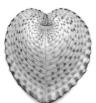

Have a heart
Prized for their beauty, most shells sold in stores have been taken as living animals. But if too many creatures are taken from one place, such as a coral reef, the pattern of life can be disrupted. Instead of buying shells, it is better to go beachcombing and collect the empty shells of already dead creatures. Always check first, since some nature preserves do not permit this.

Heart cockle shells

Oil spill
Oil is needed for industry and motor vehicles. Huge quantities are brought up from the seabed, transported in tankers, and sent along pipelines. Accidents happen where massive amounts of oil are spilled. Oil-soaked seabirds and sea mammals die of cold, because their feathers or fur no longer contain pockets of air to keep them warm.

Saving beauty
This chambered nautilus shell was carved in the 17th century. The six kinds of nautilus in the Pacific and Indian oceans are at risk from overcollecting. They are hunted at night when they rise to the surface. Chambered nautili grow very slowly, reaching maturity in six or more years, so populations can take a long time to recover.

Worse for whales

For centuries, whales have been hunted for their meat, oil, and bones. Whale oil was used in foods, as lubricants, and in soap and candles, and the broad baleen plates were made into household items such as brushes. Commercial whaling drastically reduced whale numbers. Most kinds of whale are now protected, but some are still caught for food.

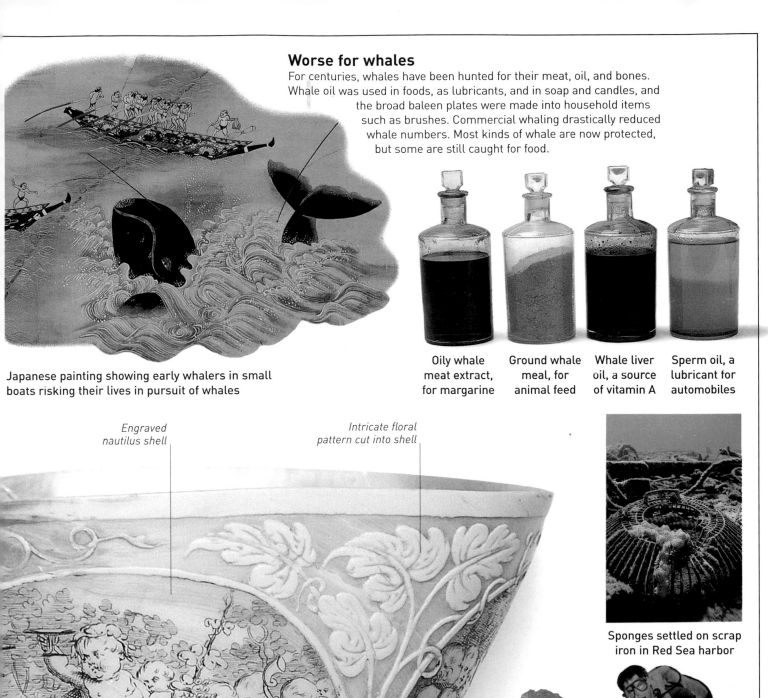

Japanese painting showing early whalers in small boats risking their lives in pursuit of whales

Oily whale meat extract, for margarine

Ground whale meal, for animal feed

Whale liver oil, a source of vitamin A

Sperm oil, a lubricant for automobiles

Engraved nautilus shell

Intricate floral pattern cut into shell

Sponges settled on scrap iron in Red Sea harbor

Take care

Sea life is fragile. A basket sponge this size may be 100 years old, but could be damaged by a diver's kick. All kinds of junk on the seabed (center, right) is smothering marine life. In the 1997–98 El Niño, sea temperatures rose by 2–4°F (1–2°C) in parts of the Indian Ocean, causing some corals to eject their algae partners and die. Many scientists think global warming may have contributed to the unusual temperature rise.

Did you know?

FASCINATING FACTS

★ The world's oceans contain 97% of the Earth's water. Of the remaning 3%, just over 2% is locked in ice, and just under 1% is freshwater.

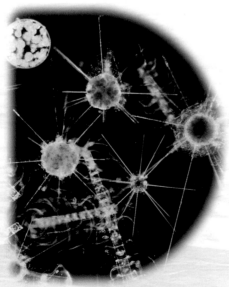

Pacific Ocean as seen from space

★ The Pacific Ocean, at 59 million sq miles (153 million sq km), covers about one-third of the Earth's surface.

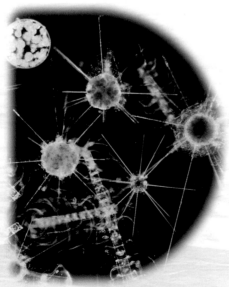

Plankton magnified several hundred times

★ The coldest sea surface is in the White Sea, in the Arctic, at 28.4°F (–2°C). The warmest is in summer in shallow parts of the Indian Ocean's Persian Gulf, at 96.1°F (35.6°C).

★ The temperature of the oceans' deepest water is between 34–39°F (2 and 4°C).

★ The highest underwater mountain is in the Pacific Ocean, near New Zealand. At 5.4 miles (8.7 km) tall, it is nearly as high as Mount Everest, Earth's highest mountain.

★ The greatest tidal range and the highest tides in the world occur in Canada's Bay of Fundy, in the Atlantic, where the difference between low and high tides can be up to 52 ft (16 m).

★ Ninety percent of all marine life occurs in the sunlit, or euphotic, zone—the surface layer of the ocean where there is enough light to support photosynthesis. Here, plankton provide the basis of the ocean's food chain.

★ A bucket of seawater can contain up to 10 million phytoplankton and zooplankton. Most phytoplankton are less than 0.0003 in (0.01 mm) wide.

★ The largest meat-eating fish is the great white shark. Some grow up to 20 ft (6 m) long and weigh around 1.65 tons (1.5 metric tons).

★ A great white shark can detect one part of blood from a wounded animal in 100 million parts of water.

★ To flee predators, flying fish can leap 6 ft (2 m) out of the water and "fly" 325 ft (100 m) on outspread fins.

Tiny cleaner wrasse at work inside the mouth of a grouper fish

★ At birth, a blue whale can weigh about 3.3 tons (3 metric tons). The babies guzzle 25 gallons (100 liters) of their mother's milk a day and grow at almost 11 lb (5 kg) an hour.

★ Small fish called cleaner wrasse feed on parasites that infest much larger fish, such as a grouper, even swimming right inside the larger fish's mouth to feed.

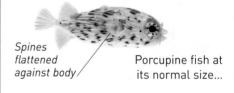

Spines flattened against body

Porcupine fish at its normal size...

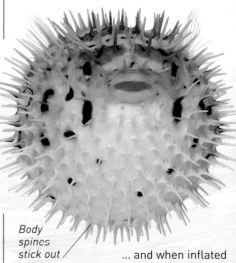

Body spines stick out

... and when inflated

★ If threatened, a porcupine fish takes in water to swell its body to twice its normal size, making it too large and uncomfortable to swallow.

QUESTIONS AND ANSWERS

Q Why is the sea salty?

A Salt is washed out of Earth's rock, sand, and soils by rainwater, then carried in streams and rivers to the ocean. Over millions of years, this has built up the ocean's concentration of salt.

Waves forming out at sea

Q What causes waves?

A Most waves are created by the wind blowing across the ocean. Their height depends on the strength and duration of the wind.

Q Why is the sea blue?

A Blue light from sunlight is the least absorbed by clear seawater. When sunlight enters the water, the blue light is scattered and some is reflected back to the surface.

Q How many types of fish are there?

A There are around 25,000 species of marine and freshwater fish. Around 24,000 are bony fish, 1,100 are cartilaginous or gristly fish and about 100 are jawless fish.

Larger upper tail vane

Tail vanes equal in size

Cartilaginous fish—blacktip reef shark (top) and bony fish—mackerel (above)

Q How do cartilaginous and bony fish differ?

A Bony fish have bony skeletons, while sharks and rays have skeletons made of cartilage (gristle). Bony fish also have a gas-filled swim bladder to control buoyancy, so they remain still. Gristly fish will start to sink if they don't keep moving. Bony fish have tail vanes of equal size and protective gill flaps, whereas most sharks have larger upper tail vanes than lower ones, and gill slits without flaps.

Stargazer hiding in gravel on the seabed

Q How do fish hide from predators in the open ocean?

A Fish that live near the surface have dark backs and paler bellies that help to camouflage them from above and below. Fish on the seabed blend in with their surroundings.

Record Breakers

★ **LARGEST SEA CREATURE**
The blue whale is the world's largest animal, at up to 100 ft (30 m) long and as much as 165 tons (150 metric tons) in weight.

★ **BIGGEST FISH**
The whale shark can grow up to 41½ ft (12.65 m) and weigh 22 tons (20 metric tons).

★ **SMALLEST FISH**
The adult Marshall Islands dwarf goby is just ¼ in (6 mm) from nose to tail.

★ **HEAVIEST BONY FISH**
The ocean sunfish, or *Mola mola*, can weigh up to 2.2 tons (2 metric tons).

★ **FASTEST FISH**
The sailfish can reach speeds of up to 68 mph (109 kph)—faster than a cheetah can run.

Whale shark

The world's oceans

There are five oceans. The Pacific, Atlantic, Indian, and Arctic oceans fill natural basins in the Earth's crust. The Southern Ocean is part of the southern Pacific, Atlantic, and Indian oceans, but is officially separate from them south of 60 degrees latitude.

PACIFIC OCEAN

The Pacific Ocean is the largest ocean, covering 28 percent of the Earth's surface. It has 20,000–30,000 islands and is surrounded by a "Ring of Fire," where tectonic activity causes frequent eruptions and quakes.

AREA: 58,957,258 sq miles (152,617,160 sq km)

Includes: Bali Sea, Bering Sea, Bering Strait, Coral Sea, East China Sea, Florest Sea, Gulf of Alaska, Gulf of Tonkin, Java Sea, Philippine Sea, Savu Sea, Sea of Japan, Sea of Okhotsk, South China Sea, Tasman Sea, Timor Sea

AVERAGE DEPTH: 13,874 ft (4,229 m)

DEEPEST POINT: 36,201 ft (11,034 m) Challenger Deep in the Mariana Trench

COASTLINE: 84,299 miles (135,663 km)

Unmanned sub reached bottom of the Mariana Trench in 1995

Kaiko submersible

CLIMATE: Strong currents and trade winds constantly blow across the Pacific's waters, often causing violent tropical storms.

NATURAL RESOURCES: Fish stocks, oil and gas fields, sand and gravel aggregates.

ENVIRONMENTAL ISSUES: Nearly half of the world's shipping routes cross the Pacific, and huge supertankers, bulk carriers, and container ships follow these routes. As a result, the ocean suffers from oil pollution, which threatens marine life and seabirds. The Pacific's endangered marine creatures include dugongs, sea otters, sea lions, seals, turtles, and whales.

Coral atoll reef in the southwest Pacific

ATLANTIC OCEAN

The Atlantic is the world's second-largest ocean, covering about one-fifth of the Earth's surface. An underwater mountain chain called the Mid-Atlantic Ridge runs down its center.

Panama Canal links Atlantic and Pacific

AREA: 31,477,905 sq miles (81,527,400 sq km)

Includes: Baltic Sea, Black Sea, Caribbean Sea, Davis Strait, Denmark Strait, Gulf of Guinea, Gulf of Mexico, Labrador Sea, Mediterranean Sea, North Sea, Norwegian Sea, Sargasso Sea, Scotia Sea

AVERAGE DEPTH: 12,391 ft (3,777 m)

DEEPEST POINT: 28,232 ft (8,605 m) Milwaukee Deep in the Puerto Rico Trench

COASTLINES: 69,512 miles (111,866 km)

CLIMATE: Northerly waters are usually covered with sea ice in winter. The Gulf Stream, a warm water current, flows from the Gulf of Mexico, north and then east, which raises the temperatures of northern Europe and keeps many northern ports ice-free during the winter.

NATURAL RESOURCES: Fish, oil, gas, sand, gravel.

ENVIRONMENTAL ISSUES: Some Atlantic waters are polluted by industrial waste, sewage, and oil. Fish stocks have run low because of overfishing, especially with trawling for bottom-dwelling fish, such as cod.

Atlantic trawler

INDIAN OCEAN

The Indian Ocean is the world's third-largest ocean. Its northern currents flow southwest along the coast of Somalia in the winter and in the opposite direction in the summer.

Endangered green turtle

AREA: 26,050,133 sq miles (67,469,536 sq km)

Includes: Andaman Sea, Arabian Sea, Bay of Bengal, Great Australian Bight, Gulf of Aden, Gulf of Oman, Java Sea, Mozambique Channel, Persian Gulf, Red Sea, Strait of Malacca, Timor Sea

AVERAGE DEPTH: 12,720 ft (3,877 m)

DEEPEST POINT: 23,376 ft (7,125 m) Java Trench, also called Sunda Trench

COASTLINE: 41,338 miles (66,526 km)

CLIMATE: Cool dry winds blow from the northeast in February and March. In August and September, southwesterly winds bring monsoon rain and flooding.

NATURAL RESOURCES: Oil and gas fields, sand and gravel, fish.

ENVIRONMENTAL ISSUES: Oil pollution; endangered sea life includes the dugong, turtles, and whales.

Oil production in the Arabian Sea

ARCTIC OCEAN

The Arctic Ocean is the world's smallest ocean. Between December and May, most of the ocean is covered by polar ice.

AREA: 3,350,023 sq miles (8,676,520 sq km)

Includes: Baffin Bay, Barents Sea, Beaufort Sea, Chukchi Sea, East Siberian Sea, Greenland Sea, Hudson Bay, Kara Sea, Laptev Sea, Northwest Passage

AVERAGE DEPTH: 6,349 ft (1,935 m)

DEEPEST POINT: 18,635 ft (5,680 m) Fram Basin

COASTLINE: 28,203 miles (45,389 km)

Steel-hulled ice breakers crush ice and open up a lane for other ships

CLIMATE: Polar, with continuous cold and narrow annual temperature ranges.

NATURAL RESOURCES: Oil and gas, sand and gravel, fish, marine mammals.

ENVIRONMENTAL ISSUES: Loss of sea ice due to climate change.

Polar bear

Partly webbed front paws for swimming

SOUTHERN OCEAN

The Southern Ocean is the world's fourth-largest ocean. Parts of the ocean freeze in winter, forming the vast Ronne and Ross ice shelves.

AREA: 8,097,843 sq miles (20,973,318 sq km)

Includes: Amundsen, Bellingshausen, Ross, and Weddell seas

AVERAGE DEPTH: 14,760 ft (4,500 m)

DEEPEST POINT: 23,737 ft (7,235 m) South Sandwich Trench

COASTLINE: 11,165 miles (17,968 km)

CLIMATE: Polar, with continuous cold and narrow annual temperature ranges.

NATURAL RESOURCES: Probable large oil and gas fields, sand, gravel, fish, krill.

ENVIRONMENTAL ISSUES: Ultraviolet radiation penetrating through the ozone hole above the Antarctic is damaging phytoplankton. Despite treaties, illegal and unregulated fishing still occurs, but protected whale and fur seal populations are making a comeback after over-hunting in the 18th and 19th centuries.

Characteristic flat-topped Antarctic iceberg

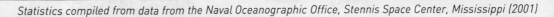

Statistics compiled from data from the Naval Oceanographic Office, Stennis Space Center, Mississippi (2001)

Find out more

There is a wealth of information available about the oceans and marine life. If you do not live (or go on vacation) near the ocean, your first stop should be an aquarium. Look, too, for excellent wildlife programs on television, or search the internet using the websites listed below as a starting point.

Razor shell encrusted with barnacles, oyster (behind), and slipper limpet

Seashells

If you visit the beach, keep an eye out for seashells washed up on shore. Bring a guidebook to help you identify them. Always put inhabited shells back where you found them and never collect shells from a protected site. Removing shells can damage the ecosystem.

Visit an aquarium

Plan a visit to an aquarium to observe a huge range of marine life from all over the world. Many aquariums have impressive viewing tanks containing hundreds of species, from jellyfish and octopuses to sharks and starfish. Look for special events where you can get close to sharks, rays, and other marine creatures.

USEFUL WEBSITES

- Join scientists on an underwater exploration:
  www.ocean.nationalgeographic.com
- Visit this site about coastal Louisiana:
  www.lacoast.gov/new/ed/KidsCorner
- Download educational presentations, plus printouts for ocean topics for grades K–12:
  www.thankyouocean.org/just-for-kids
- Find information on the world's coral reefs:
  www.reefbase.org

Study a rock pool

Rock pools are fascinating microhabitats filled with a wide variety of plants and animals. Even if you visit the same rock pool several times, it is unlikely you will find the same creatures. Look for starfish, anemones, mussels, and seaweed, such as sea lettuce and kelp. If you keep still, you may even spot crabs hiding in crevices between rocks, or see a tiny fish.

Face to face

You can see marine life up close if you take a trip in a glass-bottomed boat or a tourist submarine. Or try snorkeling—it's amazing what you can see once you're below the ocean's surface, especially if you snorkel over a coral reef.

Flukes (tail parts) of a humpback whale

Whale watching

Many companies organize whale-watching tours, giving you the chance of seeing whales in their natural environment. The tourists pictured left are observing humpback whales off the coast of Alaska.

Marine sanctuaries

Marine sanctuaries work to protect local wildlife and educate the public about marine environments. Consider planning a trip to a sanctuary or finding out more about conservation programs through the internet. You can join organizations that strive to protect and conserve the world's oceans.

Otter in the Monterey Bay National Marine Sanctuary, off the coast of California

PLACES TO VISIT

SEA WORLD—ORLANDO, FLORIDA; SAN ANTONIO, TEXAS; SAN DIEGO, CALIFORNIA

Aquatic themes include:
- seal and otter shows
- dolphin presentations
- unique exhibits at each park

NATIONAL AQUARIUM, BALTIMORE, MARYLAND

Over 100 species of marine fish showcased; features include:
- a magnificant indoor coral reef in a 335,000-gallon (1.27-million-liter) tank
- a giant Pacific octopus
- stingrays, small sharks, and sea turtles

NEW YORK AQUARIUM, BROOKLYN, NEW YORK

Exhibits feature more than 8,000 animals, including:
- exhibit on jellyfish
- animals from the Hudson River
- sea lions in the Aquatheater

SHEDD AQUARIUM, CHICAGO, ILLINOIS

At the world's largest indoor aquarium, experience:
- dolphin shows
- a coral reef exhibit
- the Pacific Northwest Coast exhibit

Pitcher from the Mary Rose

Glossary

Bioluminescence

ABYSSAL PLAIN The flat floor of an ocean basin covered in a layer of sediment. (*see also* BASIN, SEDIMENT)

ANTARCTIC Region at the South Pole, south of the Antarctic Circle.

ARCTIC Region at the North Pole, north of the Arctic Circle.

ATOLL Coral reef surrounding a lagoon, growing on the rim of a volcanic island that has sunk.

BASIN Large, natural bowl-shaped indentation in the Earth's crust. Four of the world's oceans lie in such basins.

BIOLUMINESCENCE Meaning living (bio) light (luminescence)—the production of light by a living organism. Some deep-sea creatures produce their own light. In others, it is produced by bacteria living in them.

BIVALVE Soft-bodied animal living in a hinged shell, such as a clam or oyster.

BLACK SMOKER Tall, chimneylike vent on the ocean floor that belches out superhot water containing chemicals used by some deep-sea creatures to make food. Black smokers occur at volcanically active spots on mid-ocean ridges. (*see also* MID-OCEAN RIDGE)

BONY FISH Fish such as mackerel or cod with a bony skeleton and a swim bladder to control buoyancy.

CARTILAGINOUS FISH Fish such as sharks or rays, with a cartilaginous skeleton and no swim bladder; these fish sink if they don't keep moving.

CEPHALOPOD Type of mollusk with a soft body and suckered tentacles, such as a squid or octopus.

CONTINENTAL CRUST The parts of the Earth's crust that form the continents.

CONTINENTAL DRIFT Theory that Earth's continents were once a single mass of land that slowly drifted apart over millions of years and are still moving today.

CONTINENTAL SHELF Sloping submerged land at a continent's edge.

CONTINENTAL SLOPE Sloping submerged land that descends from the continental shelf to the abyssal plain, forming the side of an ocean basin. (*see also* ABYSSAL PLAIN, BASIN)

COPEPOD Tiny, shrimplike creature, forming part of the ocean's zooplankton. (*see also* ZOOPLANKTON)

CRUSTACEAN Animal, such as a crab or krill, with jointed legs and a tough, jointed outer skeleton over its body.

Krill

CURRENT Body of water that flows through the ocean; there are both surface and deep water currents.

DARK ZONE Area of the ocean bordered by the twilight zone above and the abyss below, from around 3,300–13,000 ft (1,000–4,000 m) deep. Also called the bathypelagic zone.

DIATOM Single-celled alga and type of phytoplankton that floats near the ocean's surface, forming the basis of an ocean food chain or food web; common in cool waters.

DORSAL FIN Fin on the back of a fish that helps it keep its balance as it swims.

ECHINODERM Marine invertebrate with spines in the skin, such as a starfish.

EL NIÑO Warm water current that flows east toward the western coast of South America every few years, causing worldwide weather changes.

FOOD CHAIN Series or group of plants and animals linked by their feeding relationships. A food chain usually includes algae, or plants, plant-eating animals, and meat-eating animals.

FOOD WEB A series of several interlinked food chains.

HURRICANE Tropical storm with winds of over 74 mph (119 kph), forming over the Atlantic Ocean. Tropical storms are usually called typhoons in the Pacific Ocean and cyclones in the Indian Ocean.

ICEBERG Floating mass of ice broken off an ice-sheet or glacier, carried along by ocean currents.

INVERTEBRATE Animal without a backbone.

Swirling winds of a hurricane forming over the Atlantic

Starfish (an echinoderm)

KRILL Shrimplike crustacean that lives in Arctic and Antarctic waters in great numbers, forming much of the food supply of baleen whales.

MAGMA Molten rock that lies beneath the Earth's crust.

MARINE BIOLOGY The study of ocean life.

MID-OCEAN RIDGE Long, undersea mountain range forming where two tectonic plates are pulling apart, with magma rising from beneath the Earth's surface and hardening into rock.

MOLLUSK An invertebrate with a soft body usually enclosed by a shell. Includes bivalves (such as clams), gastropods (such as sea slugs), and cephalopods (such as squid and octopuses). (*see also* BIVALVE, CEPHALOPOD)

OCEANOGRAPHY The scientific study of the oceans.

PHYTOPLANKTON Microscopic single-celled algae that drift in the ocean's sunlit zone. (*see also* SUNLIT ZONE)

PLANKTON Tiny plant and animal organisms that drift in surface waters and are the basis of most marine food chains. (*see also* FOOD CHAIN, ZOOPLANKTON)

PLATE TECTONICS The study of the movement of the lithospheric plates that carry the oceanic and continental crust.

POLYP A sea anemone or coral with a mouth surrounded by tentacles. A hard coral polyp makes a limestone cup, or skeleton, to protect its body. Thousands of polyps live together in colonies, forming a coral reef.

ROV Short for Remotely Operated Vehicle—a small vessel operated from (and tethered to) a submersible or ship.

SALINITY The amount of dissolved salt in seawater. Salinity is measured as parts of salt per 1,000 parts of seawater; the average salinity of the oceans is 35 parts of salt per 1,000 parts of seawater.

SCUBA Stands for Self-Contained Underwater Breathing Apparatus—SCUBA divers carry their own air supply in tanks on their backs.

SEA Another word for ocean, or a particular part of an ocean—for example, the Black Sea and the Mediterranean Sea are connected to the Atlantic Ocean.

SEAMOUNT Underwater volcano that rises 3,300 ft (1,000 m) or more above the surrounding plain.

SEDIMENT Mud, sand, and silt, containing millions of tiny plants and animals, washed off the land by rivers. Sediment settles on the ocean floor.

SONAR Short for Sound Navigation And Ranging—a system that can locate the position of an object by emitting sounds then timing the echoes that bounce back.

SUBMERSIBLE Manned or remotely operated underwater research submarine designed to withstand water pressure in deep water. (*see also* WATER PRESSURE)

SUNLIT ZONE Surface layer of the ocean penetrated by sunlight, to around 650 ft (200 m) deep. Most marine life lives here. Also called the epipelagic zone.

SYMBIOSIS Close interaction between two different species where either, both, or neither benefit from the relationship.

Black smoker

TIDE The regular rise and fall of the ocean caused by the gravitational pull of the Sun and the Moon on our planet.

TRENCH A steep-sided trough or valley in the ocean floor.

TSUNAMI Sea wave usually caused by an underwater volcanic eruption or earthquake. It can cause great damage if it reaches the coast, since it may gain considerable height in shallow water. Sometimes wrongly called a tidal wave, a tsunami has no connection to the tide.

TWILIGHT ZONE Area of the ocean from around 650–3,300 ft (200–1,000 m) deep, bordered by the sunlit zone above and darkness below. Also called the mesopelagic zone.

Submersible

TYPHOON Name given to a tropical storm in the western Pacific Ocean. (*see also* HURRICANE)

UPWELLING Rising of cool, nutrient-rich water from deeper parts of the ocean to the surface, where phytoplankton and other marine life gather to feed. (*see also* PHYTOPLANKTON)

WATER PRESSURE Force exerted by water because of its weight and density; water pressure increases by one atmosphere for each 33 ft (10 m) depth.

WAVE HEIGHT The distance between the crest (top of a wave) and its trough (lowest part of a wave).

WAVELENGTH The vertical distance between two successive wave crests (the tops of the waves).

ZOOPLANKTON Tiny animals that float in the water, such as copepods and tiny crustaceans, forming part of plankton. (*see also* PHYTOPLANKTON, PLANKTON)

Index

A

abalone 59
abyssal plain 9, 10, 70; Demerara 9; Hatteras 9; Nares 9
algae 20, 22, 24, 25, 63, 70
Alvin 47
anemone, cloak 31; Dahlia 29; sea 10, 24, 29, 30, 31, 44
archeology, underwater, 54–55
Argonaut Junior 51
Asteronyx loveni 45
Atlantis, lost island of 55
Atlantis II 47
atoll 23, 24, 66, 70
Atolla 43
Autosub 53

B

bacteria 41, 43, 46, 47, 60
barnacle 38, 55, 68; goose 38
bends, the 48
Bermuda Triangle 55
bioluminescence 41, 70
bird, sea 28, 29, 38, 40, 62
bivalve 34, 35, 70, 71
blue-striped snapper 36
Botticelli, Sandro 16
Branchiocerianthus imperator 11
brittle star 6, 10, 45
bryozoan 20
buoy, monitoring 13
butterfly blenny 18

C

cable, underwater 44, 52
cephalopod 32, 70, 71
Challenger, HMS 11, 52
Chelonia mydas 39
clam 16–17, 18, 24, 30, 34, 46–47, 58, 59; sand gaper 17
climate 12–13, 26, 66, 67
coastal waters 14–15, 18
cockle, heart 62
cod 57, 66
continental drift 7, 70; shelf 8–10, 14, 70; slope 10, 70

copepod 27, 70, 71
coral 7, 10, 20, 22–25, 62–63; black 22; brain 10, 23; dead man's fingers 20; fire 22; gorgonian 23, 25; hydro- 22; organ-pipe 23; polyp 22–23, 71; reef 22–25, 29, 54–55, 62; rose 23; sea fan 22–23
Coriolis Force 12
crab 16, 17, 21, 26–27, 30–31; hermit 30–31; masked 17; pea 21; spider 21
crinoid 7
crustacean 18, 27, 30, 38, 58, 70
current 12, 38, 66, 70

DE

Darwin, Charles 23
dead man's fingers 20
decompression 48, 61
Deep Star 53
defense 30–33
diatom 26, 70
diver 48–49, 50–51, 53, 54, 61
diving bell 48; suit 49, 61
dolphin 27, 37; bottlenose 37
Dreadnought, HMS 51
dugong 16, 66
earthquake 45,55, 67
echinoderm 19, 25, 70
eel 38, 42; gulper 10, 42
Euplectellua aspergillium 45
exploration, underwater 52–53

FG

feather star 19
fish, angler- 10, 43; clown 24; craw- 18; cuttle- 30, 32; deep-sea 42–43; emperor angel- 25; flat 14; flying 10, 36, 64; grouper 53, 64; hatchet 10, 40, 41; lancet 40–41; lantern 43; lion- 32; puffer 57; porcupine 64; rat-tail 10; red band 16; sargassum 30; stargazer 65; stone- 32; tripod 10; viper 40; weever 14; wolf 28; wrasse 64

fishing 26, 56–58, 66
flounder 14
food chain 70
food web 70
fossil 6–7; fuel 60–61
Gigantura 42–43
GLORIA 52
Great Barrier Reef 23
Gulf Stream 66

HIJ

Halley, Edmund 48
hurricane 12, 70
hydroid 21; giant 11
ice 11, 67; fast 11; pack 11
iceberg 11, 54, 67, 70
jellyfish 28, 32, 33, 41, 43, 68; box 33; glass 41
jet propulsion 34–35

KL

Kaiko 66
kelp 11, 20–21
Kraken 34
lagoon, formation of 23
lateral lines 42
leafy sea dragon 8
Leptocephalus 38
lettuce slug 24–25
light organs 40–42
lobster 18–19, 30, 58; spiny 18
lumpsucker 20

M

mackerel 10, 65
maerl 32
man-of-war 10, 38
Mariana Trench 9, 47, 53, 66
Melanocetus 43
Mid-Atlantic Ridge 9, 46–47, 66
Mola mola 65
mollusk 34, 58, 71
monster, sea 19, 33, 34, 42
mother-of-pearl 58, 59
mussel 20–21, 59; date 25; horse 21

NO

Nautile 54–55
nautilus 37, 62–63
Neptune 9
Newt suit 61

Niño, El 63, 70
oarweed 10
Ocean, Arctic 8, 64, 67; Atlantic 7–9, 13–14, 26, 38, 39, 41, 44, 55, 64, 66; Indian 7–8, 24, 39, 41, 63, 64, 66, 67; Pacific 8, 11–12, 20, 24, 33, 39, 41, 47, 64, 66; Southern 8, 66, 67
octopus 10, 32, 34–35, 68; blue-ringed 32
oil and gas 60–61
Opisthoproctus 41
orange sea fan 22
overfishing 57, 66
oyster 59

PR

Palaeocoma 6
Panama Canal 66
Pangaea 7
Panthalassa 7
pearl 55, 59
Persian Gulf 64, 67
piddock 18
plankton 26–27, 28, 64, 71; phytoplankton 26, 28, 64, 67, 71; zooplankton 26–27, 64, 71
plant 10, 16, 26
plate, crustal 9, 46; Caribbean 9; North American 9; Plateau, Guiana 8
plesiosaur 7
pollution 62, 66–67
polyp 20–23, 71
predator 14, 18, 24–25, 28–29, 30, 32, 33, 36, 40, 41, 42–43
pycnogonid 44
ray 17, 33, 36–37, 65; blue-spotted 33; eagle 17; electric 36–37; reptile 7
rock 18–20, 46, 60

S

salmon 38, 56–57
salmon farming 56
salt 8–9, 11, 59, 65; farms 59
scallop 34, 35; queen 23
Scotoplanes 44
SCUBA diving 48, 50, 52–53

Sea, Arabian 8, 67; Baltic 8, 66; Bering 8, 66; Caribbean 8–9, 41, 66; Coral 8, 66; Dead 9; Mediterranean 8, 59, 66; North 60, 66; Red 8, 25, 50, 53, 63, 67; Sargasso 8, 38, 66; Tasman 8, 66; Tethys 7
sea 8–9, 71; bed 16–17, 44–45, 54–55; cucumber 10, 25, 44, 58; fan 22–23; fir 11, 21; grass 16, 58; lily 7, 19, 45; mat 20, 29; mouse 14; otter 11, 20, 66, 69; pen 10, 16, 44, 45; potato 17; slug 20, 24–25; snail 30, 31, 47, 58–59; snake 7; spider 10, 44; urchin 11, 17, 18–19, 29, 58
seahorse 17
seal 36, 38; harbor 36; elephant 36
seaweed 14, 20–21, 28, 29, 30, 32, 58
sediment 9, 71
shark 10–11, 29, 62, 65; basking 29; cat 10–11; great white 62, 64; tiger 29; whale 65
shell 30–33, 59, 62–63, 68; gaping file 33; noble pen 59
shipwreck 54–55
shrimp 27, 29, 47, 58
Siebe, Augustus 49
siphonophore 38
slate-pencil urchin 58
smoker, black 46–47, 70
snorkeling 50, 53, 69
sockeye salmon 57
sonar location 50, 52, 56, 70
sponge 10, 44–45, 58, 63; basket 63; glass-rope 44; Venus flower-basket 45
squid 10, 32, 34, 40, 58
starfish 10, 19, 25; Bloody Henry 10; crown-of-thorns 25
Sternoptyx 41
submarine 50–51
submersible 47, 50–55, 66, 71
sunstar 10; purple 19

TUV

temperature 8, 10, 13, 63, 64, 66
tidal waves 45

tides 10, 64, 71
Titanic 54
Tolossa 55
trade winds 12, 66
trawler, fishing 57
treasure 54–55
trenches 8–10, 45
trilobite 7
tsunami 45, 71
Turtle 50
turtle 7, 10, 32, 38–39, 62; green 39, 67
typhoon 12, 71
underwater exploration 48–55
Urashima Taro 39
vents 46–47; Galápagos 47
volcano 23, 45, 46

WZ

water spout 12
wave 12–13, 45, 65
weather 12–13
whale 10, 26, 27, 28, 36, 37, 38, 40, 51, 62–63, 69; blue 36, 64, 65; humpback 28, 69; killer 27; sperm 10, 40, 51
whipnose 42
wind 12–13
Wiwaxia 6
wolf fish 28
worm 14–15, 55; bristle 14; parchment 15; peacock 14–15; peanut 14; tube 15, 46, 47
zone, dark 10, 42, 43, 70; fracture 9; sunlit 10, 64, 71; twilight 10, 40–41, 71

Acknowledgments

Dorling Kindersley would like to thank:
for their invaluable assistance during photography: The University Marine Biological Station, Scotland, especially Prof. Johon Davenport, David Murden, Bobbie Wilkie, Donald Patrick, Phil Lonsdale, Ken Cameron, Dr. Jason Hall-Spencer, Simon Thurston, Steve Parker, Geordie Campbell, and Helen Thirlwall; Sea Life Centres (UK), especially Robin James, David Copp, Patrick van der Menve, and Ian Shaw (Weymouth); and Marcus Goodsir (Portsmouth); Colin Pelton, Peter Hunter, Dr. Brian Bett, and Mike Conquer of the Institute of Oceanographic Sciences; Tim Parmenter, Simon Caslaw, and Paul Ruddock of the Natural History Museum, London; Margaret Bidmead of the Royal Navy Submarine Museum, Gosport; IFREMER for their kind permission to photograph the model of *Nautile*; David Fowler of Deep Sea Adventure. Mak Graham, Andrew and Richard Pierson of Otterferry Salmon Ltd.; Bob Donalson of Angus Modelmakers; Sally Rose for additional research; Kathy Lockley for providing props;

Helena Spiteri, Djinn von Noorden, Susan St. Louis, Ivan Finnegan, Joe Hoyle, Mark Haygarth, and David Pickering for editorial and design assistance; David Ekholm–JAlbum, Sunita Gahir, Susan St. Louis, Carey Scott, Lisa Stock, and Bulent Yusuf for the clip art; Neville Graham, Sue Nicholson, and Susan St. Louis for the wall chart; Trevor Day for his assistance on the paperback edition.

For this relaunch edition, the publisher would also like to thank: Camilla Hallinan for text editing, and Carron Brown for proofreading.

The publisher would like to thank the following for their kind permission to reproduce their photographs:
a=above, b=below, c=center, l=left, r=right, t=top
Alamy Images: Paul Glendell 60tr; **American Museum of Natural History:** 11tl (no. 419(2)]; **Heather Angel** 38bc; **Ardea**/Val Taylor 62 cr; **Tracy Bowden**/Pedro Borrell: 55 tc; **Bridgeman Art Library**/Prado, Madrid 9tr; Uffizi Gallery,

Florence 16tr; **Bruce Coleman Ltd**/Carl Roessler 22c, Frieder Sauer 26tr, Charles & Sandra Hood 27tc, Jeff Foott 28tr, 56tr, Jane Burton 38bl, Michael Roggo 57tr Orion service & Trading Co. 58br; Atlantide SDF 59tr; Nancy Selton 63br, to Library: 7br; **Steven J. Cooling** 60br; **Corbis:** Jerome Sessini 60–61b, Ralph White 67c. 71bc, Roger Wood 67tr, Tom Stewart 66br; **The Deep, Hull:** Craig Guzelian 68cr; **Mary Evans Picture Library** 11tr, 12tr, 19tl, 20tl, 28tl, 33tr, 34tr, 40cl. 45tr, 48tr, 49tl, 50bl, 52tr. 54c; **Getty Images:** Nikolas Konstatinou 69tl, Will & Den McIntype 66bl; **Ronald Grant Archive** 42cl, 55bl; **Robert Harding Picture Library** 25tl, 32tr, 32bc, 39br, 57tr, 63tl; **Institute of Oceanographic Sciences:** 46lc; **Jamstec:** 66cl. © **Japanese Meteorological Agency/Meteorological Office** 12l; **Frank Lane Photo Agency**/M. Neqwman 11br; **Simon Conway Moiris:** 6tr; **N.H.P.A.**/Agence natur 44c, Linda and Brian Pitkin 67tl, Peter Parks 64bl; **National Oceanography Center, Southampton:** 53br; **Nature Picture Library:** David Shale 70tl, Doc White 65b, Fabio Liverani 65tr, Jeff Foott 69cl, Jurgen Freund 64–65, Peter Scoones 65cl, Thomas D. Mangelsen 69b; **Oxford Scientific Films**/toi de Roy 29t, Fred Bavendam 43 tl, David Cayless 68bl, 68–69, Howard Hall 64rr,

Rick Price/SAL 67b, Scott Winer 70–71; **Planet Earth Pictures**/Peter Scoones 9tl, Norbert Wu 10–11c, 20cl, 40tr, 40tl, 4lt, 42tr, Gary Bell 23br, 55tr, Mark Conlin 25c, 36br, Menuhin 29tc, Ken Lucas 30tl, NeviUe Coleman 33cr, Steve Bloom 37c, Andrew Mounter 38br, Larry Madin 43 br, Ken Vaughari 51 cr, Georgette Doowma 63cr; **Science Photo Library**/Dr. G. Feldman 26bl, Ron Church 53 cr, Douglas Faulkner 66cr, Simon Fraser 62bl, NASA/Goddard Space Flight Center 70br, Tom Van Sant, Geosphere Project/Planetary, Visions 64cl; **Frank Spooner Pictures:** 47tr, 47cr, 5/br, 54bl, 60bl, 61tr; **Tony Stone Images:** Jeff Rotman 53lc; **Stoll Comex Seaway Ltd:** 61tl; **Town Cocks Museum**, Hull 63tr; **ZEFA:** 36cl, 56ct.

All other images © Dorling Kindersley.
For further information see:
www.dkimages.com